Wood Shop

Handy Skills and Creative Building Projects for Kids

MARGARET LARSON

Storey Publishing

The mission of Storey Publishing is to serve our customers by
publishing practical information that encourages
personal independence in harmony with the environment.

Edited by Deanna F. Cook, Sarah Guare, and Nancy Ringer
Art direction and book design by Carolyn Eckert
Text production by Liseann Karandisecky
Indexed by Samantha Root Miller

Cover photography by © Jared Leeds Photography,
except front (bottom right), back (top right), and spine
(title & bottom) by Mars Vilaubi

Interior photography by © Jared Leeds Photography, except
Title (title), 4 top row center, 13 top, 15, 41 bottom, 51, 52 top,
57 left & center, 63, 78 bottom, 101, 104 bottom, 106 bottom
left, 119 bottom, 120 bottom right, 121 top left, 123, 131 top
& bottom right, 149, 151 bottom right, 168 right (both), 170
bottom, 173 middle right, and 186 bottom by Mars Vilaubi

Additional photography by © bjphotographs/iStock.com,
7 top right, 161 top; Carolyn Eckert, 83 top right, 135 right
(both), 136 bottom left, 186 top; © Coprid/iStock.com, 31
bottom right; © Dan Sherwood/Getty Images, 87 bottom
right; © efetova/iStock.com, 56 top left; © Ennessy/iStock
.com, nail icon throughout; © Frontpage/Shutterstock, 115
bottom; © GrapeImages/iStock.com, 199 bottom center;
© Nastco/iStock.com, 199 bottom right; © popovaphoto/
iStock.com, 48 bottom right (both); © Rouzes/iStock
.com, 48 top; © Rubber Ball/Alamy Stock Photo, 47 bottom
right; © scanrail/iStock.com, 56 2nd from bottom left;
© Serdarbayraktar/iStock.com, 47 top; © Steve Gorton/
Getty Images, 13 bottom, 47 2nd from top (both); © trigga/
iStock.com, 34 top

Prop styling by Caitlin Carvalho

Illustrations by Ilona Sherratt

© **2018 by Margaret Larson**

Take proper safety precautions before using potentially
dangerous tools and equipment or undertaking
potentially dangerous activities. Be alert and vigilant
while operating heavy machinery.

Storey books are available for special premium and
promotional uses and for customized editions. For further
information, please call 800-793-9396.

Storey Publishing
210 MASS MoCA Way
North Adams, MA 01247
storey.com

Printed in China by Toppan Leefung Printing Ltd.
10 9 8 7 6 5 4 3 2 1

Library of Congress Cataloging-in-Publication Data

Names: Larson, Margaret, author.
Title: Wood shop : handy skills and creative building projects
for kids / by Margaret Larson.
Description: North Adams, MA : Storey Publishing, [2018]
| Includes index. | Audience: Ages 8-12.
Identifiers: LCCN 2018021802 (print) | LCCN 2018024809
(ebook) | ISBN 9781612129433 (ebook) | ISBN
9781612129426 (paperback : alk. paper)
Subjects: LCSH: Woodwork—Juvenile literature.
| Carpentry—Juvenile literature.
Classification: LCC TT185 (ebook) | LCC TT185 .L28 2018
(print) | DDC 684/.08—dc23
LC record available at https://lccn.loc.gov/2018021802

Acknowledgments

A very special thanks to Storey Publishing, especially Deanna Cook, Carolyn Eckert, Nancy Ringer, and the wonderful publicity team.

Contents

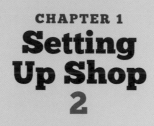
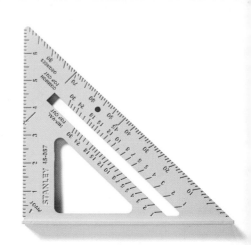

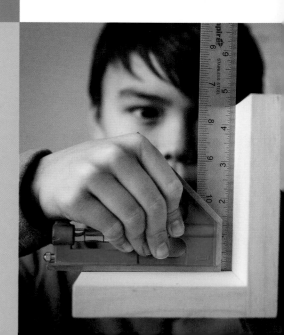

Projects

Appendix

Introduction

y earliest memory of using woodworking tools comes from elementary school, when I hammered nails into a board and then tied yarn around the nails to make a colorful design. I saved that board for years! (See String Thing on page 150 for a little blast from my past.)

I still get a thrill from making cool stuff from wood, but now I get to teach people — grown-ups and kids — how to do it too at my family's Workbench Woodworking & Craft School in Massachusetts. Our light-filled space on the first floor of an old mill building literally hums with the sounds of tools, teaching, and traditional craftsmanship.

My son, Eric, took a class at the school, in part because he really wanted to make the Sky-High Stilts (page 132). Now a teenager, he's very comfortable in the shop and has a thriving business making custom-designed cutting boards and wooden pens.

Learning the skills in this book will make you more independent, confident, and creative. You'll be able to fix things that are broken and to make things you love.

And who knows? Maybe the adults in your life will learn something too.

A NOTE TO PARENTS

For people of any age, the most thrilling part of woodworking is the projects, and we have plenty of them here for your aspiring woodworker. Our projects start with Imagination Station, where kids can explore the tools and skills they learned in chapter 2, Tool School.

The rest of the projects are divided into categories: tools and storage for the workshop, projects for indoor and outdoor fun, decor and useful things for your kid's room, and constuctions to benefit the whole house. They progress from easy to more difficult, and each comes with a list of the skills, tools, and materials your child will need.

I've also tried to give you a sense of how much each project will cost. Woodworking does require an up-front investment, but many of the projects in this book call for only one or two boards. Plus, after completing several projects, young woodworkers will have a collection of scraps that can be used for other projects. Have your child check his or her stock of lumber before you head out to buy anything new.

Many kids will want to dive right into the project that looks like the most fun, but I encourage you to have them start with the jigs on page 64. It's a low-risk, low-investment place to begin, and the builder will end up with two devices that make it easier to complete the other projects in the book.

What if you have a very young beginner? Start with String Thing or Twinkle Twinkle Star! These are easy projects with a huge "wow" factor.

And what happens when your woodworker has completed most or all of the book projects and is hungry for more? They can design their own! Ultimately, that's the goal of the book: to teach children basic woodworking and direction-following skills and to give them the confidence to apply and expand upon these new skills on their own.

PROJECT RATINGS

Skill Level: easy enough for beginners

Skill Level: experience helpful

Skill Level: for aspiring woodworkers

Cost:
$ = almost free!
$$ = moderate cost
$$$ = bring your wallet (or a generous adult!)

CHAPTER

1

Setting Up Shop

Everything you need to know

Your Workspace

Every woodworker starts somewhere, and it doesn't matter if that "somewhere" is a family workshop, a small corner of the garage, or the basement. Wherever you set up shop, keeping your tools and materials organized is essential.

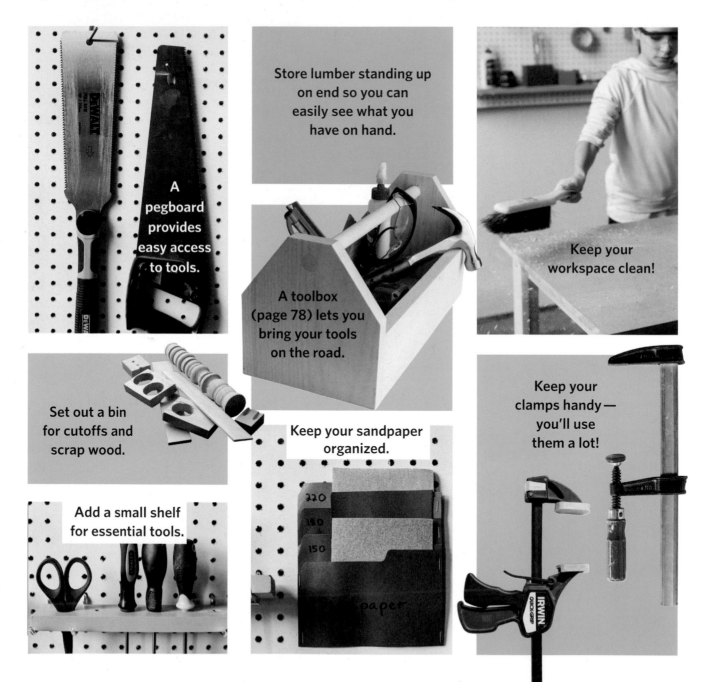

A pegboard provides easy access to tools.

Store lumber standing up on end so you can easily see what you have on hand.

A toolbox (page 78) lets you bring your tools on the road.

Keep your workspace clean!

Set out a bin for cutoffs and scrap wood.

Keep your sandpaper organized.

Keep your clamps handy — you'll use them a lot!

Add a small shelf for essential tools.

Build this
pegboard —
see page 84!

Make your own
compass —
see page 74!

Make your own
pencil holder —
see page 166!

Build this
workbench —
see page 88!

Secure long
boards
with a strap.

Build this
toolbox —
see page 78!

Your Workbench

You'll need a workbench for things like hammering, sawing, and drilling. Any sort of table will do, so long as the **benchtop** (the top of the workbench) is level, stable, and at the right height for you. If you'd like to build your own sturdy workbench, see the project on page 88.

a wood top
+
two sawhorses
=
a simple workbench

Tools & Materials

The following tools and materials will give you a great start in your workshop. You will learn all about these tools — and how to use them — in Tool School, starting on page 14.

Must-Have Tools

Pencils and a
pencil sharpener

Safety glasses

12-foot to 16-foot
tape measure

Ruler

Adjustable
combination square

Crosscut or
combination handsaw
(a combination saw
is the most versatile)

Hammer
(10 or 12 ounces to start)

Nail set

Phillips and
slotted-head
screwdrivers, each
in sizes #1 and #2

Drill

Drill bits and
screwdriver bits

Two ratcheting
bar clamps

Sandpaper
(150-, 180-, and 220-grit)

Must-Have Materials

Yellow
woodworking glue

Blue low-tack tape

1¼-inch drywall screws

2-inch common nails

2-inch finish nails

1¼-inch finish nails

1½-inch finish nails

¾-inch brad nails

Nice-to-Have Tools

Japanese handsaw
(also known as a pull saw)

Miter box and handheld miter saw

Extra clamps

Wear safety glasses or goggles whenever you're in the shop to protect your eyes.

No dangle-y things: tie back long hair and remove any dangling jewelry.

Wood Shop Safety

Woodworking tools can be sharp, heavy, or both, and they can be dangerous if you don't use them properly. The best way to prevent accidents in the wood shop is to follow a few simple rules.

Sleeves: Roll them up.

Put away tools when you're done using them.

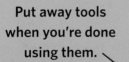

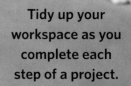

Tidy up your workspace as you complete each step of a project.

Secure boards
before using
a tool on them.

Keep sharp edges
away from yourself
and other people.

Fingers:
Watch where you
put them!

◇◇◇◇◇◇◇◇◇◇◇◇◇◇◇◇◇◇◇◇◇◇◇◇◇◇◇◇◇◇◇◇◇◇

WORKSHOP
ETIQUETTE

In your home, you know not to interrupt people
when they are talking. You'll follow a version
of that same rule in the workshop. If someone
is working with a tool, wait until they have
finished before speaking, and stay out of their
line of vision so you don't startle them.

Grown-ups should follow this rule too,
unless the woodworker is doing something
unsafe or wrong. If that happens, a grown-up
can gently place a hand on the woodworker's
shoulder and signal them to stop.

Never use a tool
as a toy.

Wear closed-toe,
sturdy shoes.
Never work in bare feet
or flip-flops.

Take your time.
You're more likely
to make a mistake
when you rush.

Learning about Lumber

What's the one thing all of the projects in this book have in common? Wood! *Lumber* is a word used to describe a piece — or many pieces — of wood. When you go to a lumberyard or home improvement store to buy lumber for your projects, you'll find it sorted by type, grade, and size.

Lumber Types

There are two basic types of wood: hardwood and softwood. Hardwood comes from trees that are deciduous, which means they lose their leaves in the winter. Cherry, maple, and oak are examples of hardwood trees. Softwood comes from trees that are evergreen, like pine trees. Most hardwoods have a higher density, or greater hardness, than most softwoods. That's why they're called hard and soft woods.

For the projects in this book, you will use pine, a softwood, because it's inexpensive and easy to work with. As your skills improve, you can "graduate" to hardwoods like cherry or maple, which have a much prettier grain.

Poplar   **Cherry**   **Maple**   **White oak**   **Pine**   **Cedar**

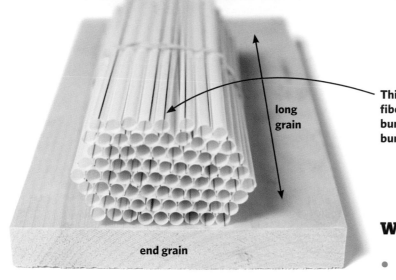

long grain

Think of wood fibers like a bunch of straws bundled together.

end grain

Glorious Grain

Grain is the orientation of fibers in the wood. You can see it in the thin, sometimes wavy lines on the face and edges of a board. The direction of grain in lumber affects how you work with it, so understanding grain will make you a better woodworker.

Imagine the set of straws above is a board. The individual straws are the fibers — or grain — in the wood. With most types of board lumber, the grain runs parallel to the edges, or long dimension, of the piece. This is called the *long grain*.

But if you look at the end of the straw "board," you'll see a bunch of hollow tubes. This is where the wood fibers were cut, letting you see the ends of the fiber cells. This is called the *end grain*.

PARTS OF A BOARD

It's important to know the proper terms for the parts of a board, since that will make it easier to understand the project instructions.

Faces = the wide, flat sides

Edges = the narrow sides

Ends = the board ends

Why does this matter?

- **Sanding direction.** You should always sand in the direction of the grain. This is called sanding "with" the grain. If you sand across ("against") the grain, you tear the wood fibers, leaving scratch marks in the wood that are very hard to remove.

- **Sawing method.** Woodworkers use different saws to cut with the grain and across the grain. When you saw across the grain, it's called *cross-cutting*. You can use a saw with lots of small teeth because you are cutting the fibers cleanly in two. When you saw with the grain, it's called *ripping*. You need a saw with fewer but larger teeth because you are splitting the fibers apart, not cutting them. For your projects, you will mostly be crosscutting, but you can use a combination saw that is good for both crosscutting and ripping.

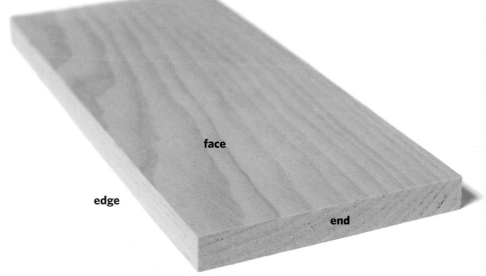

face

edge

end

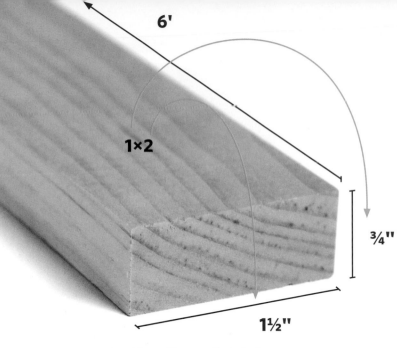

6'

1×2

3⁄4"

1½"

A 1×2 board is actually ¾ inch thick and 1½ inches wide.

LUMBER SIZES

NOMINAL	ACTUAL
1×2	¾ inch by 1½ inches
2×2	1½ inches by 1½ inches
2×3	1½ inches by 2½ inches
2×4	1½ inches by 3½ inches
4×4	3½ inches by 3½ inches
6×6	5½ inches by 5½ inches

Boards are not always cut perfectly. Always measure your lumber to get the actual dimensions.

Lumber Size

This one is a doozy. First, you should know how lumber is measured. When you see the measurement 1×2×6, the first number = thickness, the second number = width, and the third number = length. The first two numbers are in inches, and the last one is in feet.

So, you might think that a 1×2×6 board is 1 inch thick, 2 inches wide, and 6 feet long. However, those numbers actually refer to the *nominal* measurement. The nominal measurement tells you what size the board was when it was first cut from the tree, before it was planed (or smoothed) on all sides and shipped to the lumberyard. The *actual* measurement of the thickness and width is different. (See the chart at left.)

Lumber Grades

If you get grades in school, you know they are based on how well you do on a test or an assignment. Well, lumber is graded too, but it's all based on appearance.

1× lumber. Many of the projects in this book use 1× boards, like 1×2s and 1×6s. When you shop for 1× lumber, you will most likely come across two grades of pine: common and select (also called clear in some places).

- Common pine is less expensive, but it tends to have more defects, like knots (which are the points where branches joined the trunk of the tree from which the board was cut).

- Select or clear pine is more expensive but has fewer defects. I generally recommend select pine because the knots in common pine can be difficult to saw cleanly and are often visible even after the lumber is painted.

2× lumber. These boards, like 2×4s and 2×6s, are grouped by size, not by appearance. When you shop for 2× lumber, just look for boards that are mostly knot free.

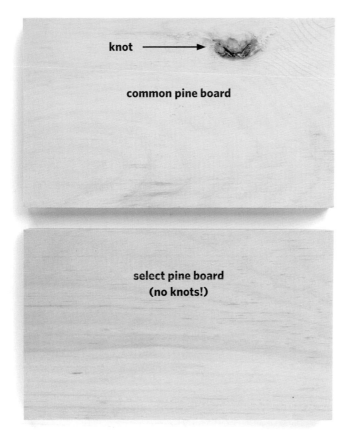

knot ⟶

common pine board

select pine board
(no knots!)

Other Lumberlike Materials

A few projects in this book call for MDF, which is a big sheet made from pressed-together wood fibers, resin, and wax. (MDF stands for "medium-density fiberboard.") You can use craft or hobby wood in place of MDF, if that's what you have. Don't use balsa wood, though; it is too light.

Some projects call for wood dowels, which are usually made of poplar and are available as round or square dowels in many different sizes at home improvement stores and craft stores.

MDF board

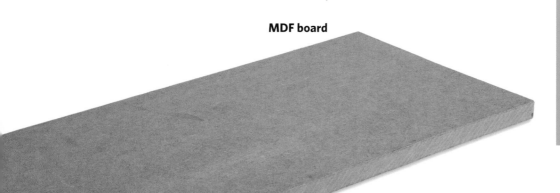

Grown-Up's Guide

Most lumber comes in 6-foot or 8-foot lengths, and MDF comes in 4-foot by 8-foot sheets. Home improvement stores and lumberyards will often cut these materials down to a more manageable size for transporting. If you buy a wider piece than you need, you will have to rip it yourself with a table saw or handsaw.

The lumber discussion is a good introduction to the raw materials used in woodworking. It gets a bit technical in spots, so you may want to revisit the topic with your child as he or she matures. Take the book along with you to the lumberyard or home improvement store to help explain some of the concepts (particularly nominal versus actual size) and make them less abstract.

CHAPTER

2

Tool School
Everything you need to know

WARNING·WEAR SAFETY·GOGGLES

Lesson 1: Layout

What You Need

➤ Ruler

➤ Tape measure

➤ Pencil

➤ Combination square

➤ Wood scraps for practice

When you measure and mark your lumber, you are working on the **layout**. Tool School starts here because that's where every project begins.

Why is layout important? Well, let's say you want to build a table. If you don't measure, mark, and cut all the table legs to the exact same length, your table will wobble. Or if you don't mark the exact right spot to put the screws that connect your table legs to your tabletop, the ends of the screws could stick out. Ouch!

MEASURE TWICE, CUT ONCE

It's the golden rule of the wood shop: Measure twice, cut once. If you always check your work by measuring twice, you'll make fewer mistakes and waste less wood and time.

Measuring

For measuring, you'll need a ruler and a tape measure. A ruler is a great tool for measuring short distances and drawing straight lines between points. A tape measure is simply a coiled-up, flexible ruler that lets you measure longer items.

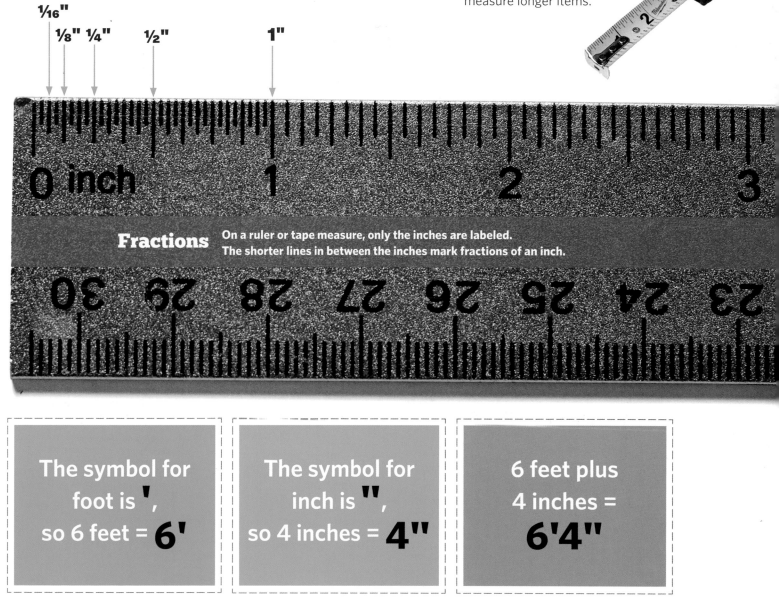

¹⁄₁₆"

⅛" ¼"

½"

1"

Fractions On a ruler or tape measure, only the inches are labeled. The shorter lines in between the inches mark fractions of an inch.

The symbol for foot is **'**, so 6 feet = **6'**

The symbol for inch is **"**, so 4 inches = **4"**

6 feet plus 4 inches = **6'4"**

Using a Square

Square is a funny name for a tool that isn't square at all. It's called that because it allows you to square a line (that is, to draw a line at a 90-degree angle to the edge of a board) or to check for square (to see if the end of a board is at a 90-degree angle to the edge or to make sure a corner is 90 degrees).

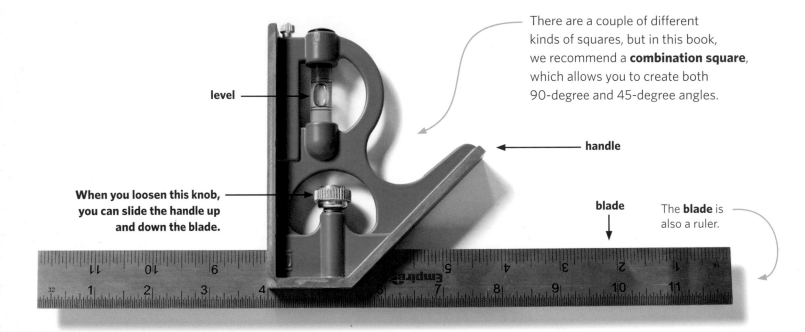

There are a couple of different kinds of squares, but in this book, we recommend a **combination square**, which allows you to create both 90-degree and 45-degree angles.

level

handle

When you loosen this knob, you can slide the handle up and down the blade.

blade

The **blade** is also a ruler.

Squaring a Line

Drawing an Angled Line

Straight side of the handle against the board

90°

45°

Angled side of the handle against the board

Hold the handle snug against the edge!

How to Check for Square

Set the 90-degree corner between the square's handle and blade over the outside corner. If the corner is square (exactly 90 degrees), you won't see any light between the board and the blade.

No light here means the corner is square!

How to Measure and Mark with a Square

Adjust the handle on the square so that its flat edge is set on the ruled blade at the measurement you want. Hold the handle tight against the edge of the board, make a mark at the end of the blade, and you're done.

To draw a line at a specific distance from the edge for the whole length of the board, do the same thing, only now slide your square and pencil along the edge of the board, marking the line.

This is the measurement you're marking.

Cool Measuring Tricks

Busy woodworkers love time-saving tips! These tricks will help you quickly measure and mark up boards without any major math work.

Divide a Board into Equal Parts

Say that you want to divide a 5½-inch board into three equal parts. Rather than trying to divide 5½ by 3 and working out that math, try this:

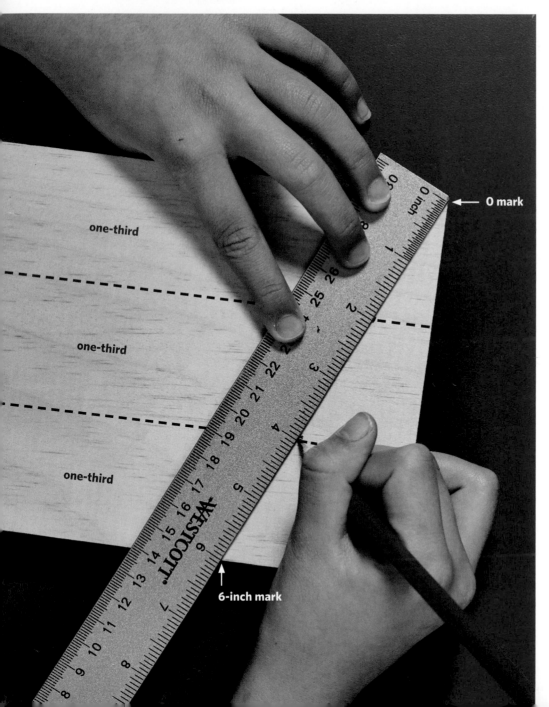

one-third

one-third

one-third

0 mark

6-inch mark

1 Choose a whole number that (1) is larger than the width of the board and (2) is easily divided by the number of parts you want. In this case, the number 6 is larger than 5½ and can be divided by 3 to make 2 (6 ÷ 3 = 2).

2 Place a ruler diagonally across the width of the board so that the 0 mark touches one edge of the board and the 6-inch mark touches the other edge.

3 Use a pencil to mark the board at 2-inch increments (that's 2 inches and 4 inches). You've now marked the board into three equal parts. The distance from the edge of the board to the nearest mark is one-third the width of the board.

Find the Center

If you need to find the exact center of a square or rectangular board, try this:

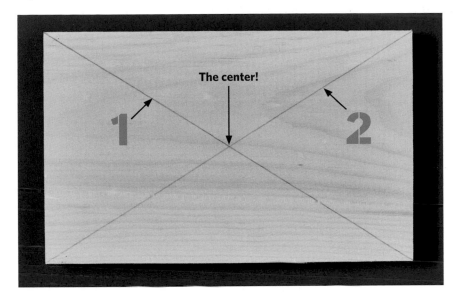

The center!

1 Use a ruler to draw a line diagonally across the board from one corner to the opposing corner. (If your board is longer than your ruler, use a straight piece of lumber.)

2 Repeat with the other two corners. Where the lines cross is the center.

Find the Middle

Let's say that you need to draw a line down the center of a board. Here's an easy way to find the middle (and to check your math!):

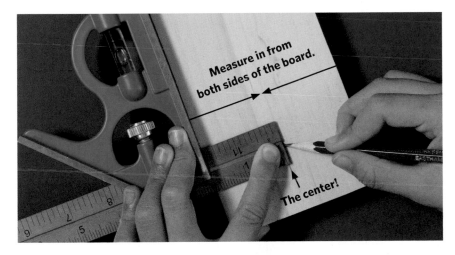

Measure in from both sides of the board.

The center!

3 Measure in from one edge of the board and make a mark at the center.

4 Repeat step 3, measuring from the other edge of the board. (If you use your combination square, you can set the measurement on the square and use it to measure from both edges — that's the quick and easy way!)

1 To begin, measure the entire width of the board.

2 Divide the width by 2 to determine one-half the total width. For example, if your board measures 3½ inches wide, half of the width is 1¾ inches.

5 Look at the two marks you made. Are they in the same spot? You might be surprised to find that the marks don't always match up, even when you measure carefully! If they don't match up, try again.

Lesson 2: Clamping

Clamps are must-have woodworking tools that act like an extra pair of hands in the shop. They're very "handy" to have around! Use them to hold your boards in place while you are sawing, drilling, or driving screws and to keep your pieces together during glue-ups.

Types of Clamps

Woodworkers like to say that you can never have too many clamps. Although there are many types of clamps, we recommend that you use ratcheting bar clamps for the projects in this book because they are easy to find and use. They have jaws with pads (to protect the wood) and a handle that slides along a metal bar. The handle has a trigger or lever that you squeeze to apply clamping pressure and a release button or lever that releases the pressure.

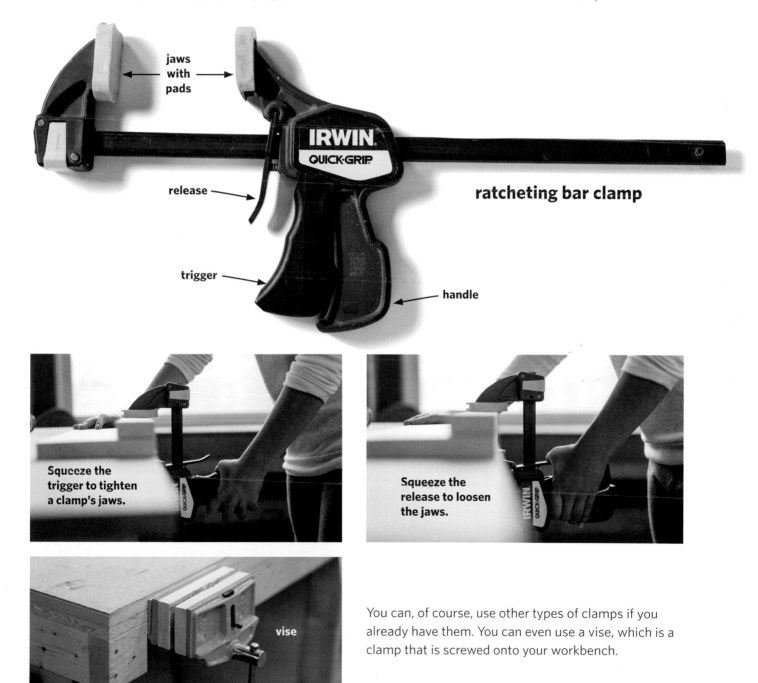

jaws with pads

IRWIN QUICK·GRIP

release

ratcheting bar clamp

trigger

handle

Squeeze the trigger to tighten a clamp's jaws.

Squeeze the release to loosen the jaws.

vise

You can, of course, use other types of clamps if you already have them. You can even use a vise, which is a clamp that is screwed onto your workbench.

Using Clamps

Whenever you wish you had an extra hand to hold a board steady, use a clamp! Use two or three! A good rule of thumb is to use as many clamps as you need to hold your boards secure while you work with them.

What will you use the clamps for?

- **Drilling holes:** Use clamps to hold your board in place. Clamp a *sacrificial board* (see below) underneath your board in case you accidentally drill too deep.

- **Driving screws and hammering:** Anytime you need your board to stay still while you work on it, use clamps!

- **Sawing:** Clamps hold your board steady while you make the cut. Here, too, a sacrificial board is helpful.

- **Glue-ups:** When you glue together two pieces of wood, you can use clamps to hold the pieces together until the glue is dry.

- **More!** You will find many, many uses for clamps in your shop.

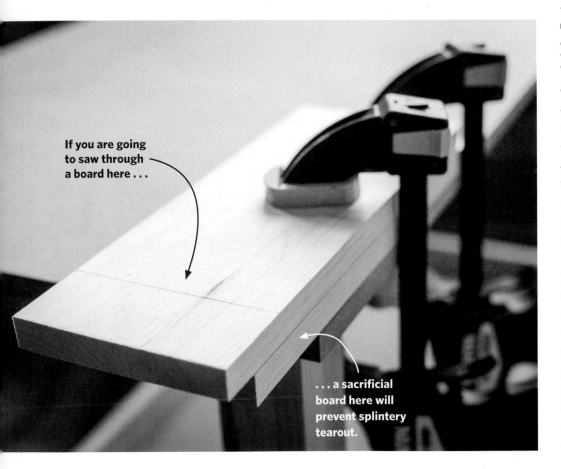

If you are going to saw through a board here . . .

. . . a sacrificial board here will prevent splintery tearout.

THE SACRIFICIAL BOARD

When you are drilling, screwing, cutting, or hammering into a board, always use a scrap piece of board underneath the board you're working on. This scrap piece is called a *sacrificial board*, and its main job is to sacrifice itself so that you don't accidentally drill, screw, cut, or hammer through your board into the surface below.

Sacrificial boards can also be used to prevent *tearout* — the little splinters that sometimes hang off a board at a spot where you've just cut or drilled. We call this tearout because the wood fibers have torn and stick out. When you clamp a sacrificial board underneath the board you are drilling or sawing, you'll still get tearout, but it will be on the sacrificial board instead of your workpiece.

Lesson 3: Sawing

Using a saw is both fun and a little tiring. You'll enjoy it more if you understand which saw works best for which type of cut, and how to use it properly.

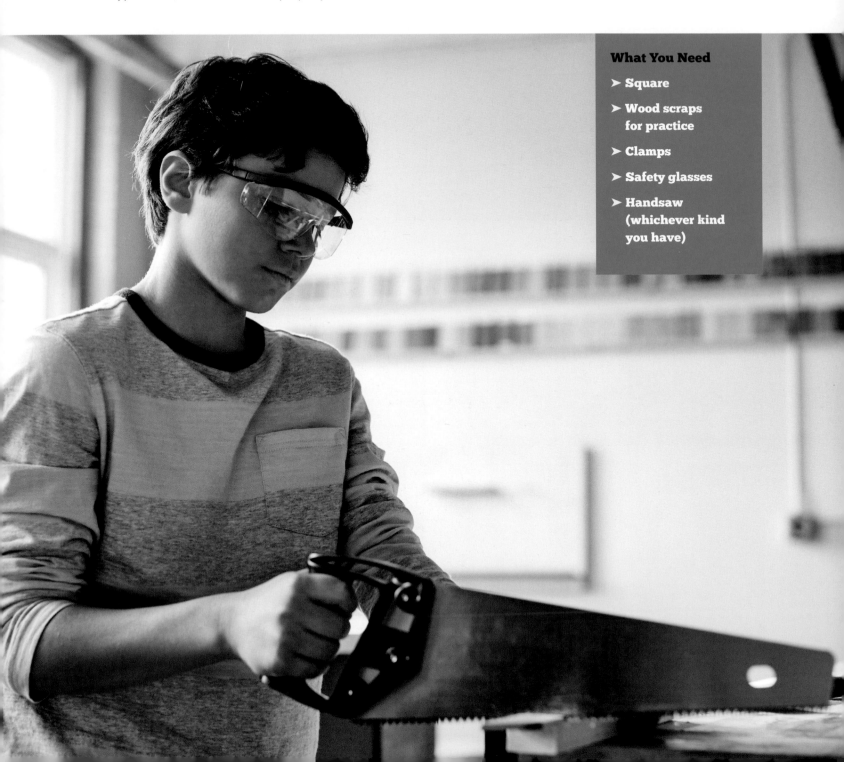

What You Need

➤ Square

➤ Wood scraps for practice

➤ Clamps

➤ Safety glasses

➤ Handsaw (whichever kind you have)

Types of Saws

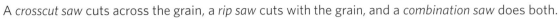

A basic **handsaw** works on the push stroke, which means it cuts when you push the saw forward.
A *crosscut saw* cuts across the grain, a *rip saw* cuts with the grain, and a *combination saw* does both.

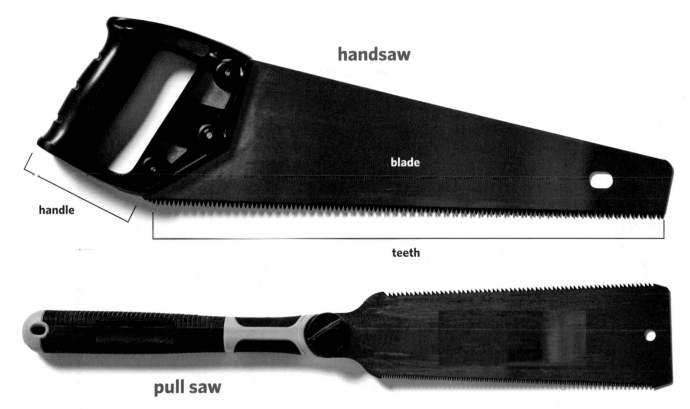

handsaw

blade

handle

teeth

pull saw

A **pull saw** is a Japanese-style saw that cuts on the pull stroke. It has a thinner, more flexible blade and is good for making fine cuts or cutting dowels.

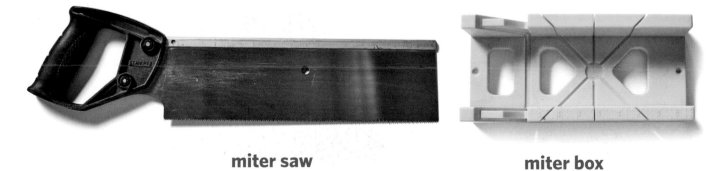

miter saw

miter box

A **miter saw** is used for making clean angled cuts. It cuts on the push stroke. If you have one, you will use it with a **miter box**, which has slots in its sides. You set your miter saw blade into a slot to help you position it at a specific angle.

How to Saw

1 **Get ready.** Use a square to mark a cut line on your board. Clamp the board onto your benchtop. You might want a sacrificial board underneath and/or a saw guide on top. Make sure that the cut line is beyond the edge of your benchtop — if you cut through the board, you don't want to accidentally cut into your workbench. Put on your safety glasses.

2 **Start the cut.** Position the teeth of the saw on the far end of the cut line and gently pull the saw toward you. Do this two or three times. Your goal is to create a small groove in the wood, which will help keep the blade from jumping out of place when you start sawing for real. Even if you have a push saw, you will pull the saw to start the cut.

3 **Saw, saw, and saw some more.** Set the saw blade in the small groove you just made. Saw with smooth, even strokes. Try not to go too fast or too hard — let the saw do the work! If you apply too much pressure, the blade may get stuck in the wood. Keep going until you have finished making the cut.

Grown-Up's Guide

Beginners often find it difficult to start their cuts, usually because they are pressing too hard or going too fast. You may have to help them with this part until they get the hang of it.

Your safety glasses are on!

Your shoulders are relaxed.

Your forearm is straight, in alignment with the blade, as you saw back and forth.

Clamp!

Set your free hand on the board to steady yourself, but away from the saw blade.

A saw guide keeps your blade on the cut line.

Clamp!

A **saw guide** — a board clamped along the cut line — can help guide your saw blade as you cut.

When you saw, the teeth act like knives and cut through the wood fibers. The space that's created by the saw blade is called the **kerf**.

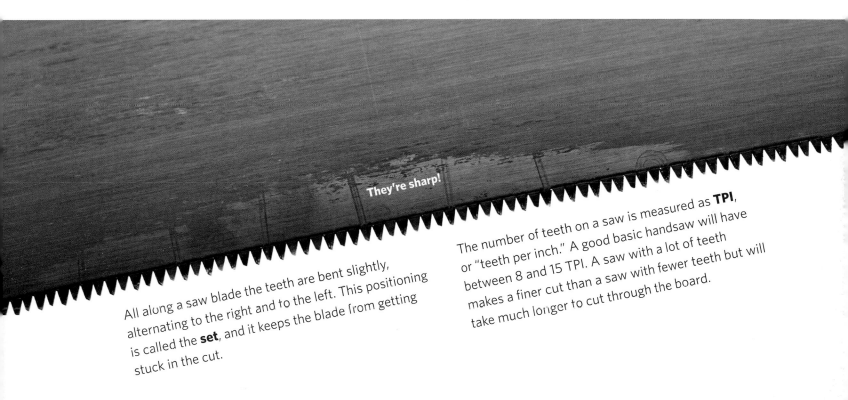

They're sharp!

All along a saw blade the teeth are bent slightly, alternating to the right and to the left. This positioning is called the **set**, and it keeps the blade from getting stuck in the cut.

The number of teeth on a saw is measured as **TPI**, or "teeth per inch." A good basic handsaw will have between 8 and 15 TPI. A saw with a lot of teeth makes a finer cut than a saw with fewer teeth but will take much longer to cut through the board.

NOTE: As you saw, think about whether the blade is cutting the wood while you push or while you pull. For efficient sawing with a push saw, you apply more pressure on the push stroke. With a pull saw, you apply more pressure on the pull stroke.

What You Need

➤ Safety glasses

➤ Drill

➤ Drill bits (twist, brad point, spade, and countersink)

➤ Clamps

➤ Blue low-tack tape

➤ Wood scraps for practice

Lesson 4: Drilling

When you use a drill, you are nibbling away at the wood to make a hole. You can do this with a hand drill, but it's faster and easier to use a cordless power drill. A power drill doubles as a power screwdriver.

chuck
where you insert the drill bit

speed control
controls the turning speed of the bit

18
16
14
12

trigger
starts and stops the drill

forward/
reverse
button
controls the
direction in which
the drill turns

power drill

handle

handle

hand drill

chuck

The projects in this book call for a power drill, but you can always use a hand drill instead. It will just take longer to drill each hole.

TOOTHPICKS TO THE RESCUE!

It's an easy fix if you drill a hole that's too small — just drill a larger one. But what if you drill a hole that's too big? If that happens, just break off or cut a few toothpicks (or wood slivers) to fit into the hole, and stick them in the hole before you insert your screws or hardware.

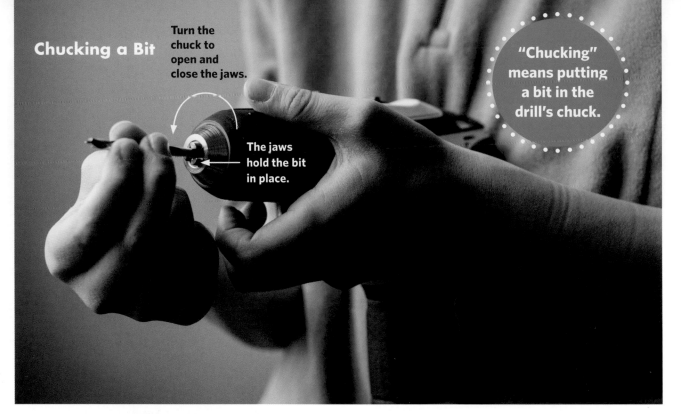

Chucking a Bit

Turn the chuck to open and close the jaws.

The jaws hold the bit in place.

"Chucking" means putting a bit in the drill's chuck.

Types of Drill Bits

Twist bits are made for drilling through metal, but they also work on wood. They can wander a bit when you start up the drill because they have no defined point at their tip to stick in the wood and hold them in place. You also get a little more tearout when you use this kind of bit.

spurs

Brad point bits have a defined point that makes it easier to start a hole. They also have sharp spurs that leave a nice clean hole.

Spade bits have a large defined point and make very large holes. When you're using a spade bit, it can be helpful to first drill a shallow hole with a smaller bit to give the spade bit's large point a place to start.

jaws

How to Drill

Using a drill is fun! Here are some tips for doing it well:

- Before you start, make sure the drill is on the forward setting!
Double-check by pressing the trigger to see if the bit turns to the right.
Set the drill to a fast speed.

- To prevent splintering, bring the drill up to full speed with just the point on
the wood, and then slowly apply pressure.

- Apply firm pressure, but let the drill do the work.

- Keep the bit straight up and down, not slanted.

- If you are drilling a deep hole, gently move the drill bit in and out of the
hole as you go to remove the *waste* (the tiny bits of wood you are removing
to make the hole).

- When the hole is deep enough, back out the bit. You don't need to use the
reverse setting. Just keep the drill running and pull it straight up out of the hole.

**Starting to drill
before bringing the
drill up to full speed
= splintery hole**

**Bringing the drill
up to full speed before
starting your hole
= clean hole**

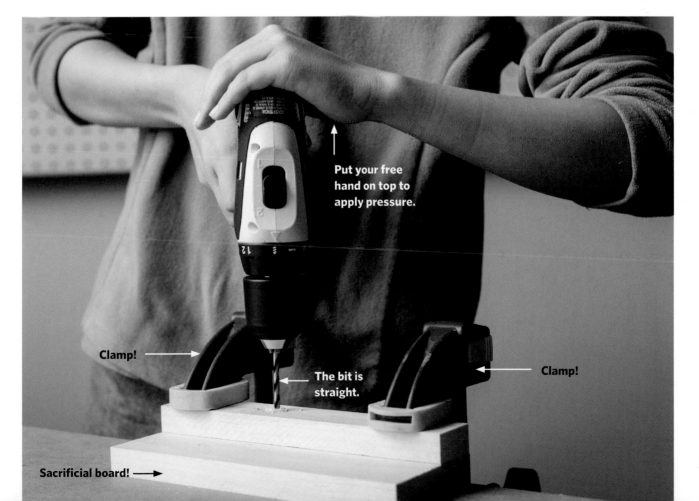

**Put your free
hand on top to
apply pressure.**

Clamp! →

← **Clamp!**

**The bit is
straight.**

Sacrificial board! →

Drilling Pilot Holes

A pilot hole is a predrilled hole — a hole you drill ahead of time — for a screw. Look at the screw you're going to drive into the wood. It has a *shank* (that's the central stem of the screw) and a *thread* (a sharp raised ridge) that wraps around the shank. To drill a pilot hole for that screw, use a drill bit that has the same diameter as the shank.

    A pilot hole keeps the wood from splitting when you drive a screw into it. Pine is such a soft wood that you can usually drive a screw into it without predrilling a pilot hole.

    You might also drill a pilot hole when you need to hammer a nail into hardwood. A pilot hole in hardwood helps prevent the nail from bending and the wood from splitting.

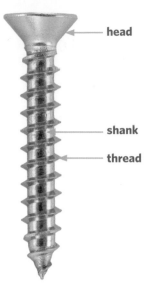

head

shank

thread

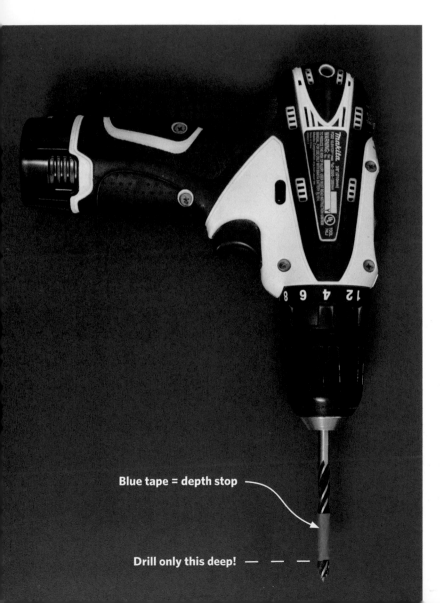

Blue tape = depth stop

Drill only this deep! — — — —

Setting a Depth Stop

Sometimes you want to stop your drill at a certain depth. For the tic-tac-toe project on page 112, for example, you want to insert the dowels only about ½ inch into the game board, so you need to drill holes only ½ inch deep.

A depth stop tells you when the hole you're drilling is deep enough. To set a depth stop, mark the depth of the hole you want right on the drill bit by wrapping a piece of blue tape around it. As you drill, stop the drill when the blue tape touches the wood.

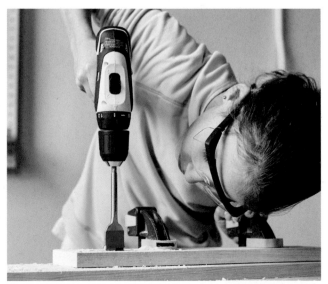

Countersinking

To **countersink** means to set the head of a screw flush with the surface of the wood. When you are drilling a hole for a screw that will be countersunk, the hole needs to be bigger at its top to make room for the head of the screw.

The countersink bits we will use in this book come attached to a regular twist bit. The countersinks are adjustable — you can slide them up or down the twist bit to set them where you want them.

And where exactly do you want to set a countersink? You need to match it to the screw you are using. Line up the screw next to your countersink bit, like it is below. Now adjust the countersink on the twist bit so that the length of the exposed bit matches the length of the shank of the screw.

When you drill the hole, drill until the countersink drives a little way into the wood — just enough that when you drive the screw into the hole, the head of the screw will sit flush with the surface of the wood.

Using a countersink is definitely a skill to practice! Practice on scrap wood with a variety of countersinks and screws. Keep practicing until you get the hang of it.

Countersink bits are numbered just like screws — #4, #6, and so on (see page 46). When you work with softwood like pine, where the head of the screw will sink easily into the wood, choose a countersink bit that's one size smaller than the screw. For example, if you are using a #8 screw, you will use a #6 countersink bit.

← countersunk hole

This screw is countersunk.

This screw is not!

Counter*sink* = a screw that is *sunk!*

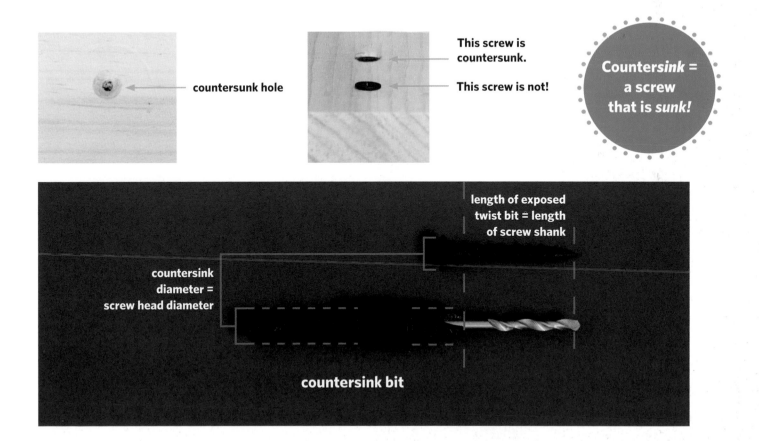

length of exposed twist bit = length of screw shank

countersink diameter = screw head diameter

countersink bit

Lesson 5:
Joinery Basics

Woodworkers use screws, nails, and glue to join together two pieces of wood. The result is called a *joint*. Joinery is the work of making joints.

Type of Joints

The projects in this book feature three types of joints: face joints, butt joints, and miter joints.

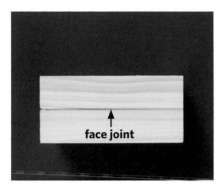

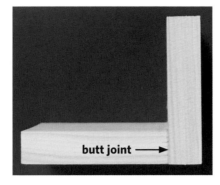

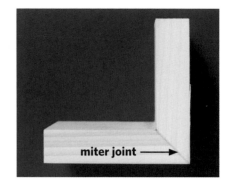

Face joint. When the faces of two boards are joined together, it's called a face joint. Once glued together, this is a very strong joint.

Butt joint. Butt joints get their name because an end or edge of one board is butted up to another board. Once glued together, an edge-to-face joint is strong, but an end-to-face joint is not, and it usually requires nails or screws.

Miter joint. This is a special type of joint where two boards are joined at an angle instead of square to each other. It looks nicer than a regular butt joint because you don't see any end grain, but it's harder to do well and it's not as strong. You will use this joint on the Mighty Message Board project (page 188).

PROUD, SHY, OR FLUSH?

Woodworkers use these terms to describe joints. A board is "proud" when it sticks out beyond a joint, and it is "shy" when it's short of the joint. A board is "flush" when it is perfectly lined up against the edge or end of another board.

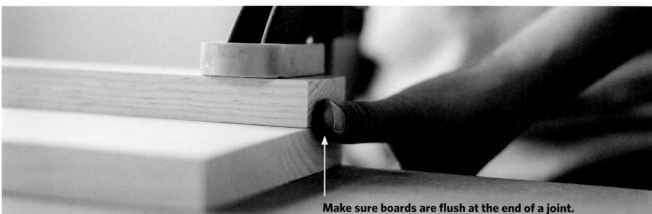

Make sure boards are flush at the end of a joint.

Lesson 6: Gluing

Woodworkers use yellow wood glue to hold joints together because it dries quickly and is easy to sand. A properly glued joint is stronger than the wood itself!

Wood glue works best on bare wood. When wood has been painted, or when you want to glue metal or other materials to wood, use hot glue, two-part epoxy, or construction adhesive under the supervision of an adult. Wood glue doesn't stick well to paint, metal, plastic, and other nonwood materials.

WOODWORKER'S TIP

If a joint is long, you can use a wallpaper seam roller to spread the glue. It does a nice job of applying the glue evenly. Plus it's easier to clean than a brush and less sticky than using your finger!

How to Glue a Joint

1 Dry-clamp your parts to make sure the joint between them is nice and tight. (*Dry-clamp* means to clamp them together without glue.) If you like, you can put a piece of blue tape along the edge of the joint to mark where it is. The tape will serve as a guide when you apply the glue.

2 Squeeze a thin line of glue on both pieces of wood at the place where they will meet. Put glue only on the places that will be joined.

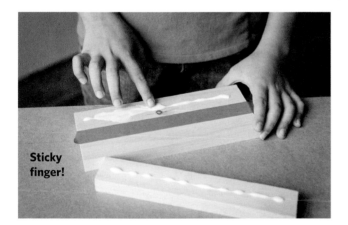

Sticky finger!

3 Spread the glue with your finger or a glue brush. This is the "Goldilocks" glue moment: not too much, not too little, but just the right amount!

4 Fit the pieces together and clamp them into place. Glue is slippery, and sometimes the boards shift out of place when you clamp them. Use your fingers to make sure that the edges and ends are flush (lined up). You have about 5 minutes to get the joint clamped. After 10 minutes, the glue will begin to harden. After 30 minutes, you can remove the clamps.

Cleaning Up Squeeze-Out

Too much

Not enough

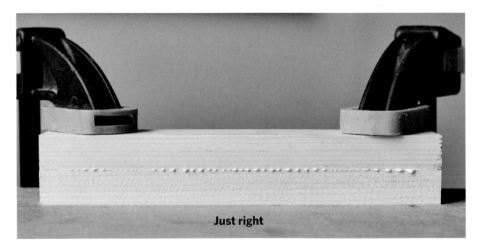

Just right

When you clamp the joint together, check for *squeeze-out*: do you see glue squeezing out of the joint? If you don't, use more glue the next time. A lot of squeeze-out tells you to use less glue the next time. A little squeeze-out tells you that you used the right amount.

If you plan to paint your project, wipe up the squeeze-out with a damp cloth, right away.

If you're going to stain your project or leave it unfinished, let the glue dry for 30 minutes or so and then scrape it off. Take care not to smear the glue. Droplets of glue will be easier to remove than smeared glue.

TIMELINE

Glue won't be fully cured, or hardened, for 24 hours, but you can remove the clamps and continue work on your project after 30 minutes so long as you don't push or pull on the glued joint.

Scraping Dried Glue

After the glued joint has dried for at least 30 minutes, touch the glue squeeze-out to see if it has hardened. If it has, you're ready to scrape. If it's not quite hard, wait another 15 to 30 minutes before scraping. If you wait longer than 1 hour, the glue will be very hard to remove and you could rip the wood fibers when you scrape it.

To scrape off the squeeze-out, slide the scraper over the glue droplets to remove them. They should peel right up. Keep the scraper blade flat against the wood so you don't gouge the wood. If the glue is smeared into the wood, you may have to use sandpaper to remove it.

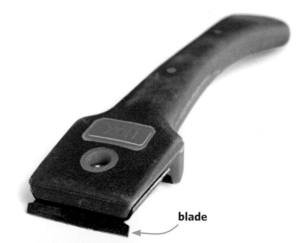

blade

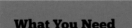

Wear your safety glasses!

When you swing a hammer, your arm should pivot at your elbow.

What You Need

➤ **Safety glasses**

➤ **Hammer**

➤ **Mallet (optional)**

➤ **Nails (common and finish)**

➤ **Nail set (optional)**

➤ **Wood scraps for practice**

➤ **Clamps**

Lesson 7:
Hammers and Nails

A hammer is a simple tool used to drive nails into wood. It takes a little strength and precision to use a hammer correctly, but it's so much fun to learn and do.

Types of Hammers

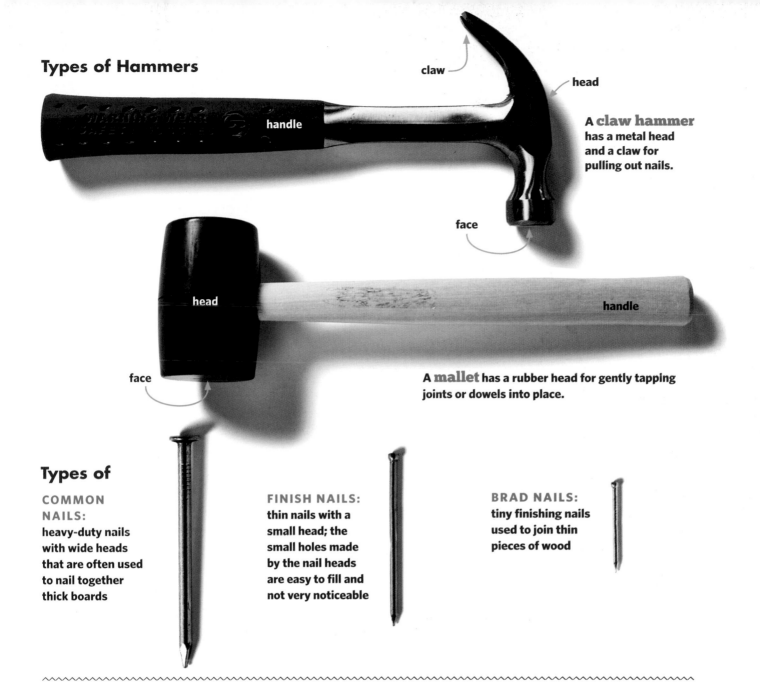

claw

head

handle

A claw hammer has a metal head and a claw for pulling out nails.

face

head

handle

face

A mallet has a rubber head for gently tapping joints or dowels into place.

Types of

COMMON NAILS:
heavy-duty nails with wide heads that are often used to nail together thick boards

FINISH NAILS:
thin nails with a small head; the small holes made by the nail heads are easy to fill and not very noticeable

BRAD NAILS:
tiny finishing nails used to join thin pieces of wood

NAIL LENGTH

Nails are measured in both inches and "pennies." For example, a 1½-inch nail is also called a 4-penny nail, which is abbreviated as 4d. This book refers to the nails by their size in inches. The boxes of nails that you buy at the store will list both inch and penny measurements.

The term "penny nail" has been around since the 1400s, when it took a certain number of pennies (or pence) to buy 100 nails. The longer the nails, the more they cost, so 100 six-penny nails cost sixpence and 100 eight-penny nails cost eightpence.

Tap gently on the nail to get it started.

Starting a Nail

Hammering a nail can basically be broken down into two parts: starting the nail and driving it home. You can then set the nail if you want, and of course if you make a mistake you can pull out the nail and start over.

Let's begin with starting a nail.

Grip the handle of your hammer with your dominant hand — that's the hand you write with. You may want to "choke up" (hold the hammer near its head) when starting a nail because it will give you better control of your hammer.

Grab a nail with your free hand, holding the nail shaft between your thumb and index finger. Set the nail point on your board. Keeping the nail straight, tap gently on the head of the nail a few times with the face of your hammer. Tap until the nail sticks into the wood and stands up on its own.

POWER TIPS

The closer your hand is to the head of the hammer, the more control you have. The farther your hand is from the head, the more power you have.

As you're hammering, the higher you swing the head of the hammer, the more power you'll have. The less you swing the head, the more control you'll have. (Whatever you do, do not swing the hammer any higher than your own head.)

As you use your hammer, you'll find a balance that works for you.

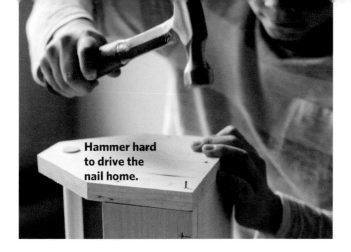

Hammer hard to drive the nail home.

Tap the nail set to drive the nail head all the way into the wood.

Driving It Home

Once the nail stands firmly on its own, remove your free hand from the nail and place it on the benchtop to steady yourself. Now swing the hammer to strike the nail hard. If the nail doesn't sink firmly into the wood as you hammer it, hit it a bit harder.

Keep hitting the nail hard until it is almost all the way in the wood. Then hit it lightly until the nail head is almost flat on the surface of the wood. Then stop. If you keep hammering the nail now, your hammer will dent the wood — usually that's not a good thing!

Setting a Nail

When you set a nail, you are sinking its head just below the surface of the wood. You do this so that the nail head won't show in your finished project. After the nail is set, you can fill the tiny hole with wood putty, then sand the putty and paint or stain over it.

What do you call a tool you use to set nails? A **nail set**, of course! Nail sets have a little tip that fits onto the nail head. You set the tip on the nail head and strike the nail set with a hammer, and it pushes the nail further into the wood.

Nail sets come in different sizes. Use a nail set that's slightly smaller than your nail head.

nail set

Bent nails happen!

Use a block for leverage and to protect the wood.

Pulling a Nail

If a nail is bent or in the wrong spot, you can use the claw on your hammer to pull it out.

Hold the hammer upside down and slide the claw underneath the head of the nail. Pull back on the handle so the claw lifts up, pulling the nail with it. If the nail is difficult to pull or you want to protect the surface of the wood, put a small block of wood underneath the hammer head. If you don't use a block, it's very easy to make a dent in the wood with the head.

Lesson 9: Sanding

Imagine a bunch of little rocks glued to a piece of paper. That's basically what sandpaper is. When the sandpaper is rubbed over wood, the rocks (called particles) help remove splinters and smooth out the surface. Sandpaper is often listed as a material but is really a tool for removing wood (in teeny-tiny amounts).

Grit

Sandpaper is classified by *grit*, which describes the number of particles per square inch on the paper. A low grit number means the particles are fewer but bigger, and a high number means the particles are more numerous but smaller. In other words, a lower number means a rougher sandpaper.

Low-grit sandpaper removes a lot of wood quickly but leaves the sanded surface scratched and somewhat rough. **High-grit sandpaper** removes less wood and leaves the surface smooth, so it's ready for paint or stain.

Grits range from 24 to 2,000, but for the projects in this book you will use 150-grit, 180-grit, and sometimes 220-grit sandpaper.

220-grit

180-grit

150-grit

How to Make a Sanding Block

A sanding block is an essential woodworking tool. It's simply a piece of wood that you wrap sandpaper around, gritty side out. A sanding block makes it easy to sand the surface of a wood board evenly and smoothly.

1 Cut a 4½" piece from a 1×3 board.

2 Sand the block, "breaking the edges" — gently sanding the edges to round them — on just one face.

3 Write "Sanding Block" on the face with the rounded edges so you'll know that's the side that you'll put your hand on.

4 Wrap a piece of sandpaper, gritty side out, around the bottom side of the block, and you're ready to start sanding!

broken edge is rounded

To "break the edge" of a board, gently sand the edge until it is smooth and slightly rounded, rather than a sharp corner.

How to Use Sandpaper

Sanding a board may seem like no big deal, and it's not, provided that you follow two simple rules:

Start with the lowest grit and move up.
When you use sandpaper, you are scratching the wood surface to remove minor imperfections. If you have a magnifying glass, you can actually see the small scratches. When you move up in grit, you replace that first set of scratches with smaller, finer ones. Eventually, the scratch marks will be too small to see and the wood surface will be nice and smooth.

Sand *with* the grain. Sanding with the grain leaves you with a nice smooth surface. If you sand against the grain, you will break the wood fibers and create scratches that are hard to remove. Take care not to sand in an arch across the wood. We call this "banana sanding," and it's a no-no.

Sand *with* the grain.

Banana sanding — it's ugly!

53

Lesson 10: Finishing

Some kids love to decorate their projects, while others like the look of natural wood. There's no right or wrong way. Finish the project however you like!

What You Need

➤ Paint or stain
➤ Brushes
➤ Rags

Pick the Right Finish

If you want to finish your project with paint or stain, first sand it well and wipe it free of dust. Before applying any finish, test it on a piece of scrap wood to make sure you like it.

All of the projects in this book suggest using pine, which is a very soft wood. While that makes it easy to work with, it means that the wood dents easily. Pine will show every flaw when it is stained, which is fine if you like the rustic look. Paint, on the other hand, will cover the small flaws and can be as colorful as you want.

At right is a piece of pine with four different finishes: paint, two different kinds of stain, and a clear coat of protective urethane. You can see how different each finish looks.

In the end, your choice of finish is up to you. Whatever you do, be sure to:

Sand and wipe your project clean before finishing it.

Cover your work table with newspaper or plastic to protect it.

Follow all the safety precautions listed for your choice of finish.

Apply your finish in two or more thin coats, letting it dry after each application. It will stick — and look — better than if you apply it in one thick coat.

Brown latex paint

Walnut gel stain

Walnut polyurethane stain

Clear urethane

Lesson 11:
Imagination Station

 ow that you've learned how to use your new tools, you can practice your skills as you design and build your own unique creations.

Although many of the projects in this book can be customized, they are still someone else's idea and design. This is your chance to take inspiration from your raw materials and see where they lead you. The best part is, you can return to this section any time for ideas to spark your imagination as your woodworking skills improve and your confidence grows.

FINDING SCRAPS

If you don't yet have any wood scraps, you can ask for some cutoffs at a home improvement store or lumberyard. You'll find more interesting scraps by visiting a local maker of fine furniture or a cabinetmaker. They are usually happy to give away their scraps, especially if a young person asks.

What Do I Need?

All your tools. Fasteners, like nails, screws, bolts, washers, and glue. Scrap wood, dowels, twigs — any kind of wood you can find! Finishes, like paint, plus stickers, yarn, glitter, and whatever other crafty stuff you have lying around. This is no-holds-barred imagineering work!

Where Do I Start?

Look around for inspiration. What catches your eye? Maybe it's a building or a tree. Or maybe it's an animal or a person's face.

Look in an art book or a children's picture book. What about that amazing sculpture? Or this strange Dr. Seuss character?

Look at your toys. Your action figures, dolls, or stuffed animals might need a hideout, a bridge, or furniture!

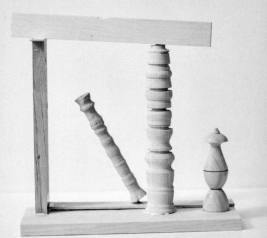

What Do I Do?

That's what you get to decide! Once you've dreamed up what you'd like to build, look through your materials and start fitting things together. Need a smaller piece? Saw one to size. Drill some holes, glue some parts together, and sand all the edges to make it fancy. You can even add other materials you find around the house (like washers or fabric that can be glued to the wood, or cool stickers).

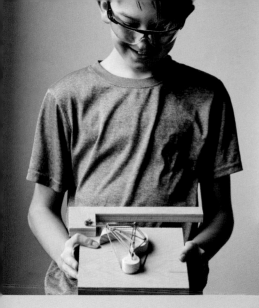

Idea Factory

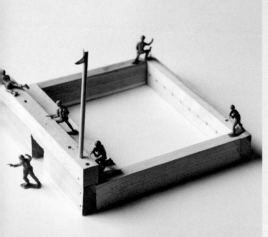

CHAPTER

3

Workshop

Projects to get your shop up and running

Sawing Jigs

Skill Level:
Cost: $

A jig is a device that helps hold and guide your tools. Jigs come in handy when you need to work with unusual shapes or want to repeat a task easily and accurately. Woodworkers often have many different jigs in their shops, and some can be used for more than one task.

This project shows you how to make two jigs for sawing. The narrow stock jig helps you hold dowels and other thin pieces that can be hard to clamp or hold while you're cutting them. (*Stock* is just a fancy name for lumber.) The crosscut jig helps you hold and cut larger dowels or wider lumber, giving you a nice, straight cut every time.

What Do You Need?

TOOLS

Safety glasses

Layout tools

Clamps

Power drill

#4 countersink bit

#2 Phillips screwdriver bit

Handsaw

Permanent marker

MATERIALS

1   12-inch length of 1×2 select pine board

1   12-inch length of 1×4 select pine board

12   1¼-inch coarse-thread drywall screws

2   18-inch lengths of 1×3 select pine board

1   18-inch length of 1×6 select pine board

Grown-Up's Guide

Jigs are often made with scrap lumber. For the narrow stock jig, for instance, you need a 12-inch piece of 1×4 and a 12-inch piece of 1×2. If you don't have scraps, you can buy narrow stock, or you can rip (saw lengthwise) wider lumber to make the narrower stock.

Older kids might find a larger jig more comfortable. They could use a 1×3 or 1×4 on top of a 1×6.

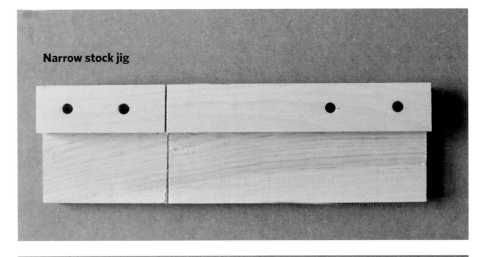

Narrow stock jig

Crosscut jig

NARROW STOCK JIG

1×2

1×4

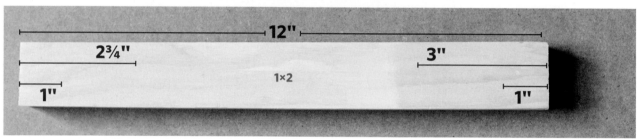

12"

2¾"

1×2

3"

1"

1"

Assemble the Jig

1 Measure and mark the locations of the four screws on the 1×2 board, following the diagram above. Center the marks on the face of the board.

2 Place the 1×2 board on top of the 1×4 board so that both ends and the bottom edges line up. Clamp the boards together on your bench.

3 Chuck your drill with the #4 countersink bit and set it to a depth of 1¼ inches (see page 34 for instructions). With the drill running at high speed, drill a pilot hole at each of the four marks on the 1×2.

4 Chuck your drill with the #2 Phillips screwdriver bit. With the drill on low speed, drive in four of the 1¼-inch screws to fasten the 1×2 to the 1×4.

Cut the Kerf

1 Measure 4 inches in from the right side of the jig and mark the spot on the 1×2. Square a line across the 1×2 at that spot.

2 Using your handsaw, carefully cut along the line you just marked, stopping as soon as you've cut through the 1×2.

3 Almost done! The last step is to use a permanent marker to label your jig "narrow stock" so you know what it's used for. You can add more kerfs later for other projects, if you want.

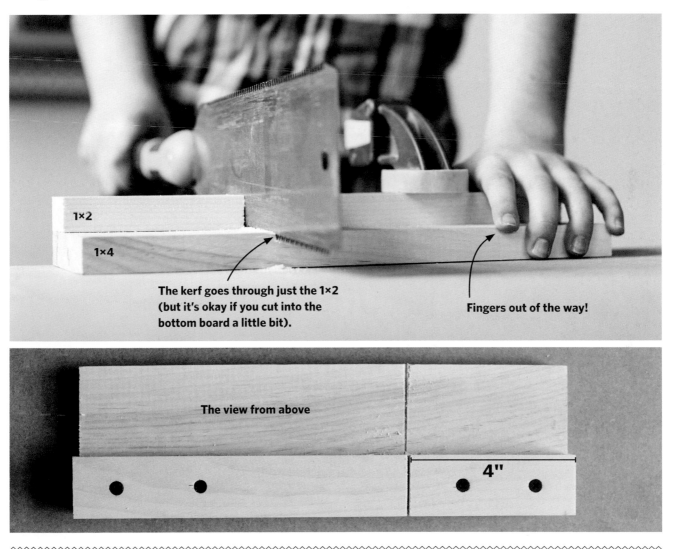

1×2

1×4

The kerf goes through just the 1×2 (but it's okay if you cut into the bottom board a little bit).

Fingers out of the way!

The view from above

4"

LEFT-HANDED?

If you're a lefty, the narrow stock jig will work better for you if the kerf is on the left side. Instead of measuring 4 inches in from the right to mark the cut line, measure 4 inches in from the left and make the cut there.

CROSSCUT JIG

Assemble the Jig

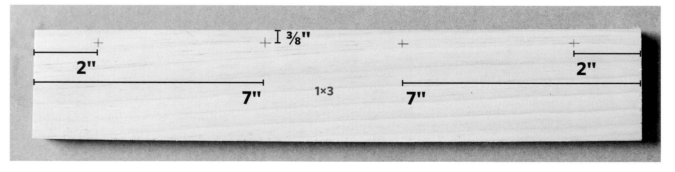

2"

7"

3/8"

1×3

7"

2"

1 Measure and mark four holes for screws on both 1×3 boards, following the diagram above.

NOTE: The spots you are marking on the 1×3 boards are where you will drive screws through the boards into the edges of the 1×6 board. The 1×6 board is ¾ inch thick, so the center of that edge is at ⅜ inch — and that's where you are marking spots for the screws to go.

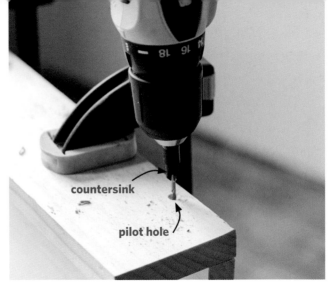

2 Clamp one of the 1×3s to the 1×6 as shown above, aligning them on the ends and edges. Use two clamps to keep the boards stable. Ask a grown-up or a friend for help if you need an extra set of hands.

3 Chuck your drill with the #4 countersink bit and set it to a depth of 1¼ inches (see page 34 for instructions). Drill a pilot hole at each of the four marks.

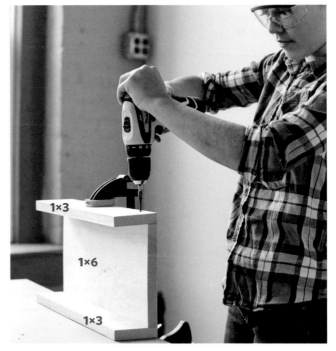

4 Chuck your drill with the #2 Phillips screwdriver bit. With the drill on low speed, drive a 1¼-inch screw into each hole to fasten the 1×3 to the 1×6.

5 Repeat steps 2, 3, and 4 to screw the second 1×3 board to the opposite edge of the 1×6.

Using Your Jigs

1 Clamp your jig to the bench.

2 Set the board you are cutting on the jig, aligning the cut line on the board with the kerf in the jig.

3 Hold the board firmly against the side of the jig with one hand, or clamp it in place.

4 With your other hand, set your saw blade in the kerf and make the cut.

Over time, the saw blade movement will eventually make the kerf too large to be useful. When that happens, just cut a new kerf. When you run out of room for new kerfs, it's time for a new jig.

Clamp!

The kerf in the jig guides the saw blade.

Setting a Stop on Jigs

If you are cutting a board into a lot of equal lengths, you can set a stop on a jig to mark the length that you want to cut.

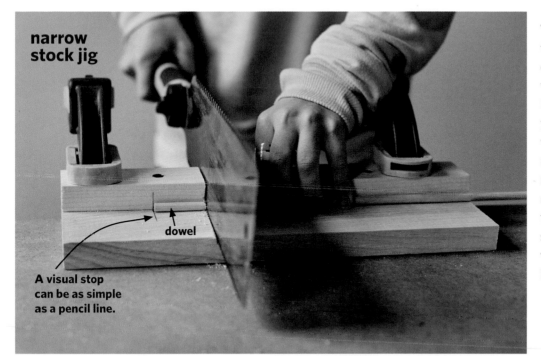

narrow stock jig

dowel

A visual stop can be as simple as a pencil line.

Visual stop: Mark the jig at the desired distance from the kerf with a small penciled line or blue tape on your jig. Slide the wood or dowel to meet the line, then make the cut. This is recommended only for very narrow stock, since thicker stock will be harder to hold in place by hand.

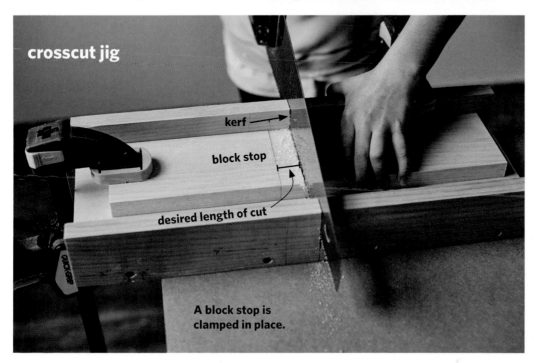

crosscut jig

kerf →

block stop

desired length of cut

A block stop is clamped in place.

Block stop: Clamp a piece of wood at the desired distance from the kerf. For example, if you needed to cut a board into a lot of 3-inch lengths, you could clamp a small piece of wood in the jig 3 inches from the kerf. Slide the board down to meet the block stop, then make the cut. Repeat as needed. This gives you 3-inch lengths with no need to measure and mark each cut.

Clever Compass

You've learned how to draw perfectly straight lines, but what if you want
to draw a perfectly round circle?

A compass is a tool for drawing circles of many different sizes. The kind you can buy in a store
has two arms joined by an adjustable elbow, with one arm that ends in a point and one arm that
holds a pencil. But you can also make your own compass, and it's even simpler and easier to use.
It can draw circles of up to 12 inches in diameter and will come in handy for projects like
String Thing (page 150) and Clock Time (page 182).

What Do You Need?

TOOLS

Safety glasses

Layout tools

Clamps

Hammer

Power drill

$\frac{1}{16}$-inch drill bit

$\frac{7}{64}$-inch drill bit

Fine felt-tip permanent marker

MATERIALS

1   7-inch length of ¼-inch-thick × 1¼-inch-wide lattice strip or flat trim

Small brad nail or push pin

Sandpaper (150-grit)

Making the Compass

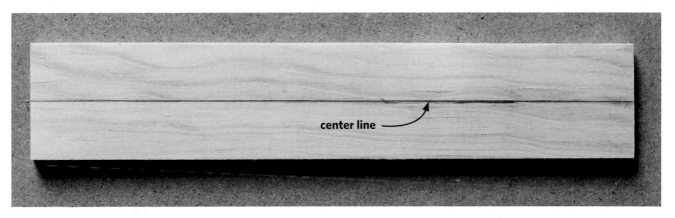

center line

1 Measure the width of the lattice strip, then divide that number in half to find the center of the strip. Mark the center at each end of the strip. Draw a straight line down the length of the strip to connect the two marks.

NOTE: You can use your narrow stock jig (page 66) for cutting the compass strip to length.

Making the Compass *continued*

2 Hook a tape measure over one end of the strip, stretch it out 7 inches, and lock it so it stays in place. Make a mark ½ inch in from the end of the strip, marking right on the center line. Label this mark "0."

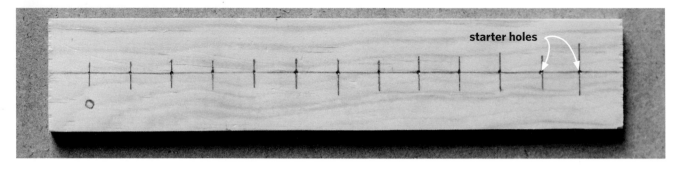

3 Make a mark every ½ inch, starting at the 0 mark and moving down the strip. You should have 13 marks total, including the 0 mark.

4 Clamp the strip to your workbench with a sacrificial board underneath. Using a hammer and a small nail, gently tap the nail at each mark to make a shallow starter hole.

5 Chuck your drill with the ¹⁄₁₆-inch bit and drill a hole through the strip *only* at the "0" mark. The material is thin so it won't take long!

6 Chuck your drill with the ⁷⁄₆₄-inch bit and drill a hole at each of the remaining marks.

7 Lightly sand the compass, then use the permanent marker to label your holes. The first hole is 0, then ½ inch, 1 inch, 1½ inches, and so on, until you get to 6 inches for the last hole.

Using Your Compass

1 Place your compass on your paper, board, or whatever surface you're going to draw a circle on. Put the 0 hole at the spot where you want the center of your circle to be. Push or lightly hammer a push pin or brad nail through the 0 hole and barely into the wood below.

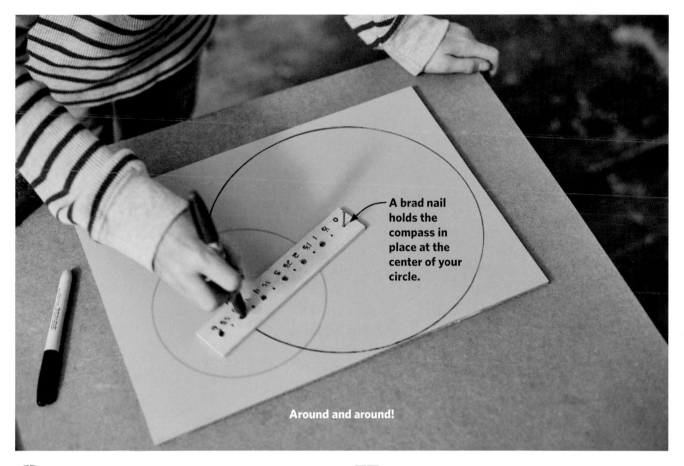

A brad nail holds the compass in place at the center of your circle.

Around and around!

2 Set the tip of a pencil or pen in one of the holes, holding it straight up and down. Carefully swing the compass around, keeping your pencil or pen on the board or paper below, until you've made a complete circle.

3 Practice a few more times with different holes so that you're comfortable using your new compass.

NOTE: You can mark and drill holes for your compass every ¼ inch if you want a more precise compass. You can also use a lattice strip or trim piece that is longer than 7 inches if you want a bigger compass. The 7/64-inch holes are the right size for a sharp pencil, but you can drill bigger holes if you want to use a marker with your compass.

Tool Tote

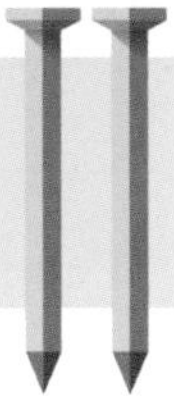

Every woodworker needs a place to store their tools, and this tote does the job! Make a second one to use for craft or school supplies.

What Do You Need?

TOOLS	MATERIALS	
Safety glasses	2	7½-inch lengths of 1×8 select pine board
Layout tools	2	13½-inch lengths of 1×4 select pine board
Clamps		
Handsaw	1	13½-inch length of 1×6 select pine board
Power drill		
⅛-inch brad point drill bit	1	15-inch length of ¾-inch wood dowel
¾-inch spade drill bit		
Hammer	20	1¼-inch finish nails
Nail set		Wood glue
Mallet		Sandpaper (150- and 180-grit)

Exploded View

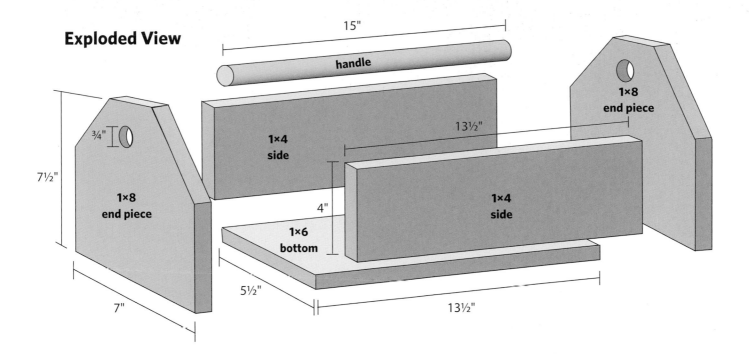

15"

handle

7½"

¾"

1×8
end piece

7"

1×4
side

5½"

1×6
bottom

4"

13½"

13½"

1×4
side

1×8
end piece

Cut the End Pieces

1 Measure, mark, and square a line 7 inches across the *width* of both 1×8 boards. The line should be about ¼ inch in from one edge. Clamp each board to your bench and rip it along the line. A saw guide — a board clamped along the cut line to help guide your saw blade — will help make this difficult cut a bit easier. The boards will now be 7 inches wide and 7½ inches long.

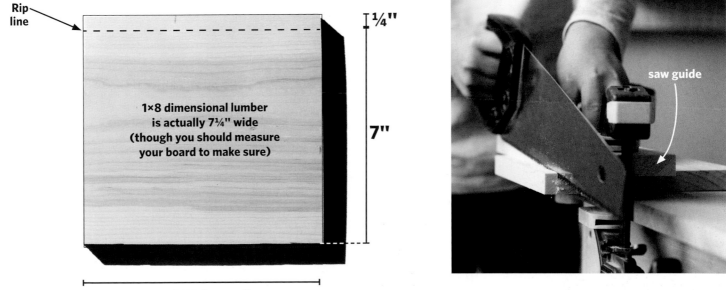

Rip line

¼"

1×8 dimensional lumber
is actually 7¼" wide
(though you should measure
your board to make sure)

7"

7½" length

saw guide

Cut the End Pieces

continued

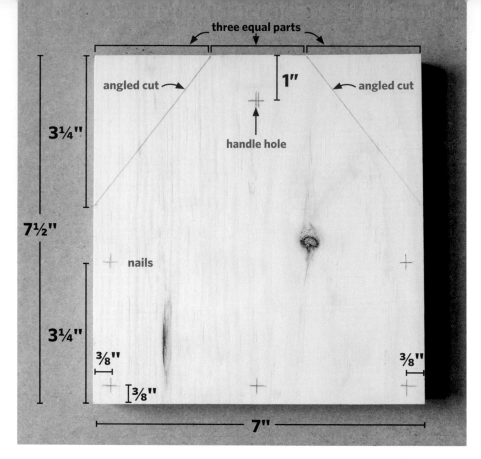

three equal parts

angled cut → →**angled cut**

1"

handle hole

3¼"

7½"

3¼"

+ **nails**

⅜" ⅜"

⅜"

7"

2 Divide the 7-inch width of each board into three equal parts, using the trick on page 20. Then mark each 7- × 7½-inch board as shown. You are setting up the angled cuts for the end pieces of the tool tote.

3 Clamp each board to your bench and saw along the lines, using a saw guide again, if needed.

4 Clamp one of the end pieces on top of a sacrificial board. Chuck the drill with the ⅛-inch brad point bit and drill a shallow pilot hole at the handle hole mark to give the spade bit a place to start. Chuck the ¾-inch spade bit and drill the hole at the mark, letting the drill get up to speed first and clearing the sawdust as you go.

5 Repeat to drill a handle hole through the second end piece.

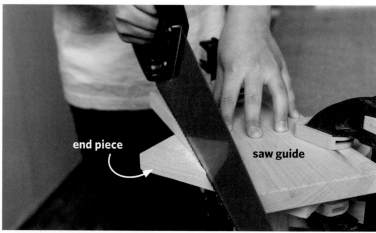

end piece **saw guide**

Attach the Sides

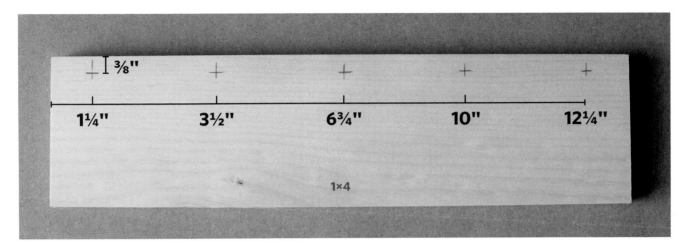

3/8"

1¼" 3½" 6¾" 10" 12¼"

1×4

1 Mark one edge of a 1×4 board — measuring from the left — as follows: 1¼ inches, 3½ inches, 6¾ inches, 10 inches, and 12¼ inches. Use your square to mark ⅜ inch up from the bottom edge at each spot. This is where your nails will go.

2 Repeat the markup on the second 1×4 board. These two boards will be the sides of your toolbox.

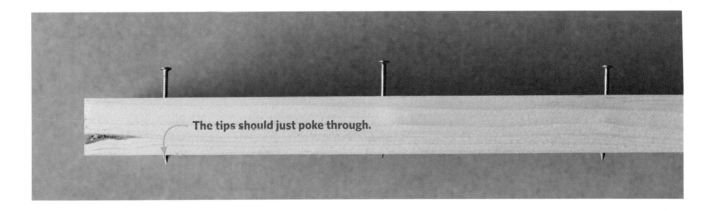

The tips should just poke through.

3 At each of the spots you just marked, hammer in a finish nail so it just barely pokes through the wood. The points of the nails will help the sides stick to the base so they don't slide around when you glue the pieces together.

Attach the Sides *continued*

1×4 side

glue along
this joint

support block

1×6 bottom

4 The 1×6 board will be the bottom of your toolbox. Set it up on one edge. Set one of the 1×4
side boards against the 1×6, with the nail points on the
edge of the 1×6. Set a block of some kind — a scrap
piece of 1×6 will work — under the opposite side of the
1×4 side piece. Dry-fit the boards, pushing the parts
together so the nails indent the wood, and check to
make sure the corners will align well.

5 Pull the two boards apart, apply glue to both
parts at the joint, and fit them back together.

6 Hammer in the finish nails.
Use the nail set to countersink the nails.

7 Repeat steps 4 through 6
to nail the second 1×4 side
board to the 1×6 bottom board.

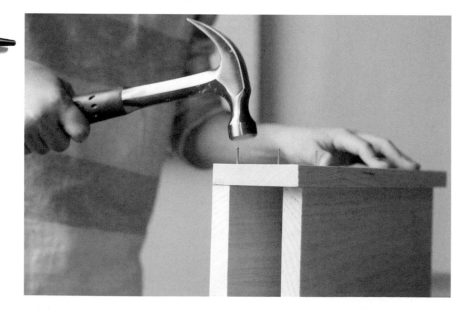

Attach the End Pieces and Handle

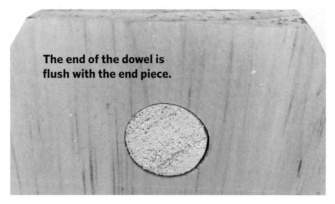

The end of the dowel is flush with the end piece.

1 At each of the nailing spots you marked on the end pieces, hammer in a finish nail so it just barely pokes through the wood.

Take just *one* of the end pieces and repeat the same dry-fit/glue/hammer/countersink steps you did on the side pieces to attach the end piece to the base and side pieces.

2 Apply a little glue to one end of the dowel. Slide the glued end into the ¾-inch hole on the attached end piece. Use the mallet to tap the dowel flush with the outside face of the end piece.

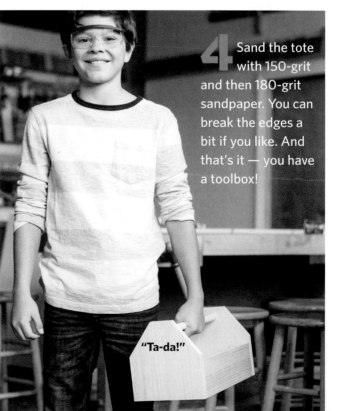

3 Apply glue to the remaining end piece and to the other end of the dowel. Fit the end piece over the box so the dowel goes into the ¾-inch hole. Tap the end piece with the mallet until the dowel is flush with the outside of the end piece. Hammer in the nails in the end piece, and set them with the nail set.

4 Sand the tote with 150-grit and then 180-grit sandpaper. You can break the edges a bit if you like. And that's it — you have a toolbox!

"Ta-da!"

Storage Pegboard

This pegboard will come in handy for organizing your tools and supplies. You'll need a piece of pegboard that is 2 feet by 4 feet. If you can't find it in that size, you can have pegboard cut to size at the lumberyard or home supply shop where you buy it.

What Do You Need?

TOOLS	MATERIALS	
Safety glasses	2	23½-inch lengths of 1×2 common or select pine boards
Layout tools		
Clamps	8	1½-inch finish nails
Hammer	2	46-inch lengths of 1×2 common or select pine boards
Power drill		
#2 Phillips screwdriver bit	Wood glue	
#4 countersink bit (optional)	1	2- × 4-foot piece of pegboard
	14	1¼-inch coarse-thread drywall screws

Make the Frame

23½"

1 On each end of the 23½-inch boards, measure and mark two spots ⅜ inch in from the end and each edge. These eight marks will show you where to set the nails when you construct the frame.

⅜" ⅜"

⅜"

⅜"

2 Hammer a finish nail on each mark so that the ends just poke through the other side of the wood.

46" board

Glue!

3 Apply glue to both ends of one of the 46-inch boards. Clamp it to the bench so that it is standing on one edge.

4 Set one 23½-inch board on its edge, with the nail heads facing out. Align the end of this board with the clamped 46-inch board. Press the boards together, then hammer the nails home. Repeat on the remaining three corners to complete the rectangular frame.

NOTE: After you've nailed the frame together, go around and check all the nails to make sure they're still sunk. Sometimes nailing on one side of a board can cause a nail on the opposite side to pop out a little bit. If you find any nails that have popped out, drive them back home.

Attach the Pegboard

1 Lay the frame on your bench. Place the pegboard on top of the frame.

2 Feel with your fingers to center the pegboard over the frame. It doesn't have to be perfect, but the frame should be completely hidden by the pegboard. When you're happy with the alignment, clamp the setup to your bench.

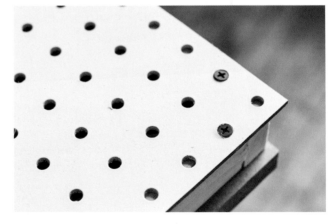

3 Chuck your drill with a #2 Phillips screwdriver bit. Starting in one corner, drive two 1¼-inch drywall screws through the holes in the pegboard and into the frame. Repeat on the remaining corners.

4 Drive a few additional screws along each side to secure the pegboard in place.

NOTE: If no holes in the pegboard match up with the frame, use a #4 countersink bit to drill pilot holes through the pegboard and into the 1×2 frame for the screws.

Hang your new pegboard at a height that makes it easy to reach your tools. Ask a grown-up for help if you need it.

You can buy special holders for your screwdrivers, but why not make your own? Start with double pegboard hooks and then cut a 1×3 to size and drill the holes.

Or skip the holes and make a nice long shelf to hold all those small items that are easily lost.

Outline each saw in your collection for easy clean-up

Personalize your pegboard by adding your initials or name. You can make the letters with paint, letter stickers, washi tape, or whatever you like.

Idea Factory

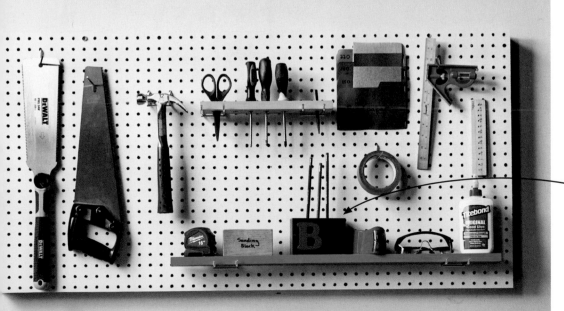

Don't forget to build a custom-size DIY Pencil Holder (page 166) to hold your pencils!

My Own Workbench

Skill Level:
Cost: $$$

Imagine having your very own bench! This one offers plenty of space for work and includes a shelf for storing supplies. Plus, the legs can be removed and replaced with taller legs to make the bench higher as you grow. The benchtop also can be replaced when it starts to show wear and tear.

If you're new to woodworking, you can have these parts cut to size at a lumberyard or home improvement center and just assemble it at home. If you have more experience, you can cut all the parts yourself.

This project can take a while to assemble because there are lots of glue joints that need time to dry. You can speed up the process if you have a lot of clamps so you can glue more than one joint at a time.

Exploded View

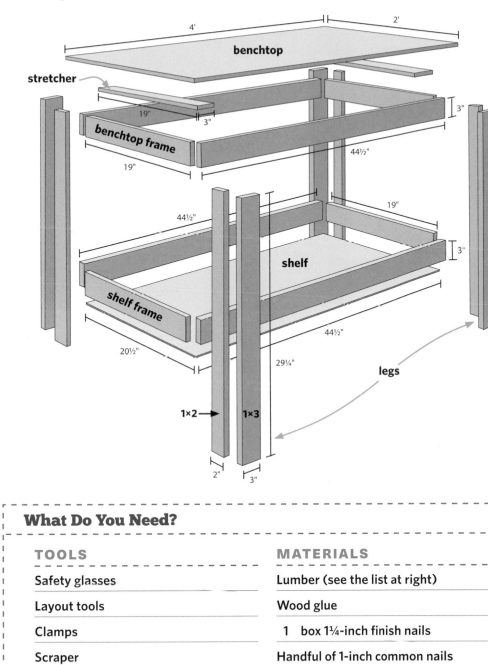

4'

2'

benchtop

stretcher

19"

3"

3"

benchtop frame

19"

44½"

44½"

19"

shelf

3"

shelf frame

44½"

20½"

29¼"

legs

1×2

1×3

2"

3"

NO WORRIES

You'll be doing a lot of nailing and screwing on this project. So what if you make a mistake and put a fastener in the wrong place? Just remove it and try again! You don't even have to patch the holes. It's okay to make mistakes here.

You'll be banging up the workbench soon enough, so don't worry if it's not perfect.

LUMBER

LEGS

4   29¼-inch lengths of select pine 1×2 boards

4   29¼-inch lengths of select pine 1×3 boards

SHELF FRAME AND BENCH TOP FRAME

4   19-inch lengths of select pine 1×3 boards

4   44½-inch lengths of select pine 1×3 boards

SHELF

1   20½- × 44½-inch sheet of ¼-inch MDF

BENCH TOP

1   2- × 4-foot sheet of ¾-inch MDF

STRETCHERS

2   19-inch lengths of select pine 1×3 boards

SCRAP LUMBER FOR ASSEMBLY

2   18-inch lengths of board lumber (any width)

What Do You Need?

TOOLS

Safety glasses

Layout tools

Clamps

Scraper

Hammer

Power drill

¼-inch brad point drill bit

#2 Phillips screwdriver bit

MATERIALS

Lumber (see the list at right)

Wood glue

1   box 1¼-inch finish nails

Handful of 1-inch common nails

24   1¼-inch coarse-thread drywall screws

Sandpaper (150-grit)

Assemble the Legs

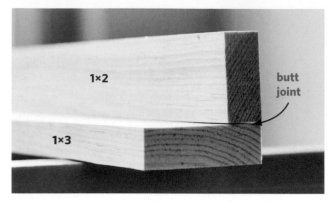

1 Place one 29¼-inch 1×3 board on your work surface. Place one 29¼-inch 1×2 board on top to make a right-angle butt joint, as shown above. Check the dry-fitted joint to make sure the edges and ends align well.

2 Separate the boards. Apply a line of glue to the bottom edge of the 1×2, where it will attach to the 1×3. Spread it evenly with your fingers.

3 Fit the two boards back together, aligning their outer edges, and clamp them together. Let the glue dry for at least 30 minutes, then scrape off any excess squeeze-out.

4 Repeat steps 1 through 3 to assemble the other three legs.

Build the Shelf Frame

1 You'll need a stable work surface for these next steps. Since you're in the middle of building a workbench, let's assume that you don't already have one! For now, you can set your future benchtop — the 2-foot by 4-foot piece of ¾-inch MDF — on sawhorses (or any other sturdy support). You can also work right on the floor of your garage or on a driveway.

2 For the shelf frame, you'll need two of the 44½-inch 1×3s and two of the 19-inch 1×3s. Set them on their edges to form a rectangle, as shown above.

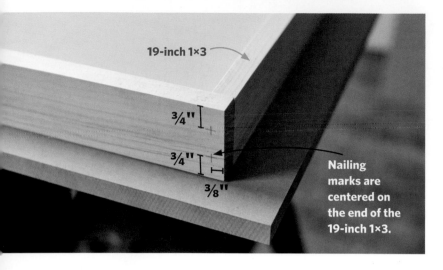

19-inch 1×3

¾"

¾"

⅜"

Nailing marks are centered on the end of the 19-inch 1×3.

3 Lay the 44½-inch boards flat on your work surface. At the end of each board, measure and mark two nailing spots: ⅜ inch in from the end, and ¾ inch from the top and from the bottom. Set the marked boards back in place and check that the nailing marks are centered on the ends of the 19-inch 1×3s.

4 Clamp one of the 44½-inch boards with one end on top of a sacrificial board. Set another board under it, in the middle, to keep it level. Drive a 1½-inch finish nail at each mark so the ends of the nails are just poking through the other side of the board. Repeat on the other end of the board. Repeat the process on the second 44½-inch board.

5 Now you are ready to hammer the frame together:

- Put the four boards back in the frame configuration. Dry-fit each corner, pressing the tips of the nails in as you make sure the edges of the boards are aligned.

- Disassemble the frame and apply glue to both parts of one of the corner joints, spreading it with your fingers. Be careful around those nail tips!

- Press the joint together.

- Clamp the 19-inch 1×3 that you will be driving nails into.

- Hammer in the nails the rest of the way.

6 Repeat the gluing, clamping, and hammering to complete the remaining three corners of the shelf frame.

Assemble the Shelf

¼-inch MDF

⅜ inch

1 Set the ¼-inch piece of MDF on your work surface. Set your combination square to ⅜ inch, and use it to draw a line ⅜ inch in from the edge around the entire perimeter. This is your nail guide.

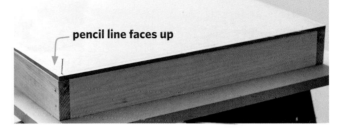

pencil line faces up

2 Apply glue to the top edges of the shelf frame and spread it with your fingers or a brush. You do not need to put glue on the MDF.

3 Set the MDF on top of the frame, lining up all the corners. The side with the line penciled in around the perimeter should be facing up.

4 Pick a corner. Make sure that the MDF lines up perfectly with the frame there, and then hammer in a 1-inch common nail at that corner.

5 On that same long edge, move to the second corner and drive another nail. Repeat the process on the other side of the shelf.

6 Hammer a nail in the center of each side. Then put in nails every 3 inches or so along each side. When you're done, set the shelf aside for now.

glue joint faces up

leg assembly

sacrificial board

Install the Legs

1 Clamp one leg assembly to the edge of your work surface on top of a sacrificial board, with the glue joint facing up.

11½"

1" 1⅜"

9"

1x2

1⅜" 1" 1"

1⅞"

2 Measure and mark the leg's 1×2 (which is now on top) at four spots, as shown above, for drilling holes for screws. The screws are offset (not in a straight line) so that they will connect the pieces more securely.

3 Chuck the drill with a ¼-inch drill bit and drill through the wood at all four marks. Repeat the same process to mark up and drill a second leg assembly.

1"

1" 1⅜"

1⅞"

11½"

1⅜" 1"

9"

4 Clamp a third leg assembly in place on the sacrificial board, again with the glue joint facing up. Measure and mark the leg's 1×2 as shown above.

5 Drill through the wood at four marks. Repeat the same process to mark up and drill the fourth leg assembly.

6 Now you're ready to attach the legs to the benchtop:

a. Set one of the four legs on top of the MDF benchtop. Make sure that the glue joint on the leg is on the shorter side of the bench. This way, you won't see the glue joint from the front.

b. Clamp the leg to the frame.

c. Chuck your drill with a #2 Phillips screwdriver bit. Use the drill to drive two 1¼-inch drywall screws through the holes you drilled in the leg and into the benchtop frame.

d. Unclamp, then repeat the same process to attach the other three legs.

glue joint is on short side

short side of bench

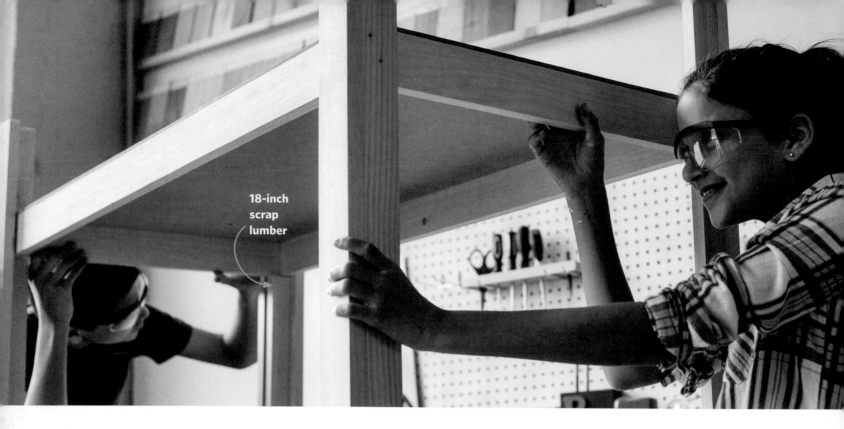

18-inch
scrap
lumber

Attach the Shelf to the Legs

Now comes the interesting part! You definitely need a helper for this, so go find someone who can lend a hand.

1 Your bench should still be upside-down at this point. Set the two 18-inch pieces of scrap lumber standing straight up in opposite corners of the upside-down bench. These will hold the shelf up while you attach it to the legs. With your helper, set the shelf assembly on top of the scrap-wood supports, with the MDF side facing up.

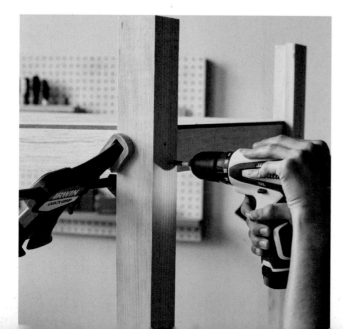

2 Clamp the shelf frame to the leg at one of the corners that is supported by scrap lumber. Screw in two 1¼-inch drywall screws through the predrilled holes in the leg and into the shelf frame. Unclamp, then repeat the same process at the opposite corner, where the other scrap wood support is.

3 Now that you've secured two of the legs, remove the scrap wood supports and move them to the other two corners of the shelf frame. Clamp and screw the remaining two legs to the shelf frame in the same way.

Whew! You're Done!

Set the bench upright on the ground. Sand any rough spots until they are smooth to the touch. Then move the bench to its new home and start using it!

PLAY IT SAFE

The shelf of your new workbench will hold your tools and supplies. Although it looks like a cozy place to hide, it's not built to hold the weight of a child. So treat it like any other woodworking tool and use it for its intended purpose.

NOTE: If the floor in your workspace is uneven, your bench may rock while you're using it. In that case, put a furniture self-leveler (which you can buy at any home supply store) on the bottom of each leg.

Fun & Games

Just build and play!

Easy-Up Tent

Some woodworking projects don't take long at all. You can build this awesome indoor/outdoor tent in about an hour. Throw a blanket over it and you have your own private space for reading or relaxing. Don't forget the matching Tiny Tent (see page 111) for your dolls or stuffed animals!

Exploded View

Skill Level:
Cost: $

What Do You Need?

TOOLS

Safety glasses

Layout tools

Clamps

Power drill

⅛-inch brad point drill bit

¾-inch spade drill bit

Mallet

Paintbrush (optional)

MATERIALS

6 48-inch (4-foot) lengths of 1×2 clear or common pine board

Sandpaper (150-grit)

Spar varnish (optional)

3 48-inch (4-foot) lengths of ¾-inch wood dowel

Blanket, sheet, tablecloth, or sewn fabric

Make the Tent Frame

1 Measure the width of your 1×2 boards and divide by two. Our boards are 1½ inches wide, so the width divided by two is ¾ inch. On each board, measure and mark drilling spots ¾ inch in from each end and centered across the width (which should be at ¾ inch in from the edge).

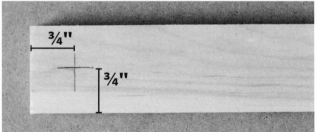

¾"

¾"

2 Clamp one board on top of a sacrificial board, letting them both hang a couple of inches off the bench. The sacrificial board will prevent tearout when you drill a hole through the board.

3 Chuck your drill with the ⅛-inch bit and drill a pilot hole in the center of your marked cross to give the spade bit a place to start.

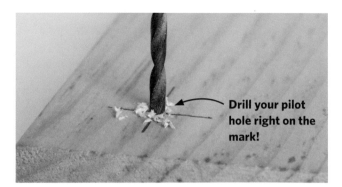

← **Drill your pilot hole right on the mark!**

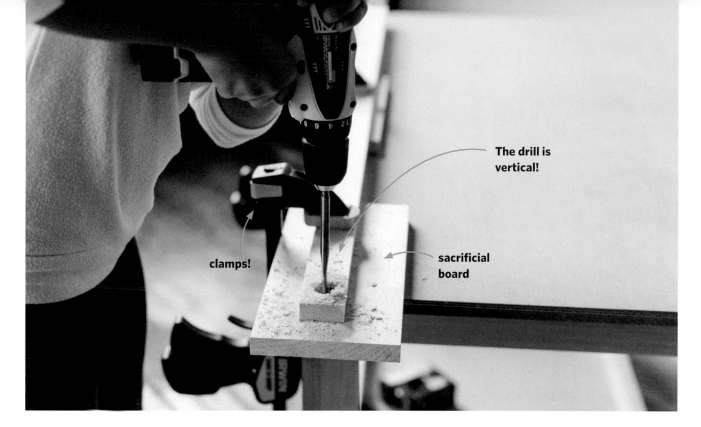

The drill is vertical!

clamps!

sacrificial board

4 Chuck the drill with the ¾-inch spade bit. Put the tip of the spade bit in the pilot hole. Start the drill and let it get up to speed before plunging it into the wood. Carefully move the bit up and down as you drill to clear out the sawdust.

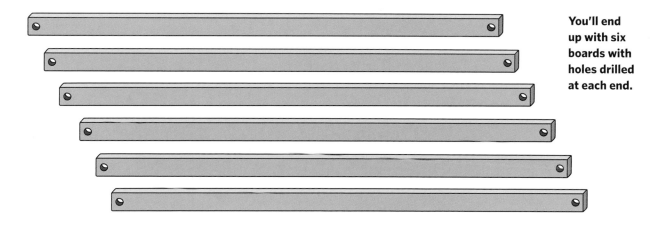

You'll end up with six boards with holes drilled at each end.

5 Drill the other end of the board the same way. Then repeat to drill holes on both ends of the remaining five boards.

6 Sand all the edges of the boards so they are smooth.

7 If you plan to leave your tent outside for a while, finish all the wood parts with spar varnish.

Assemble the Tent Frame

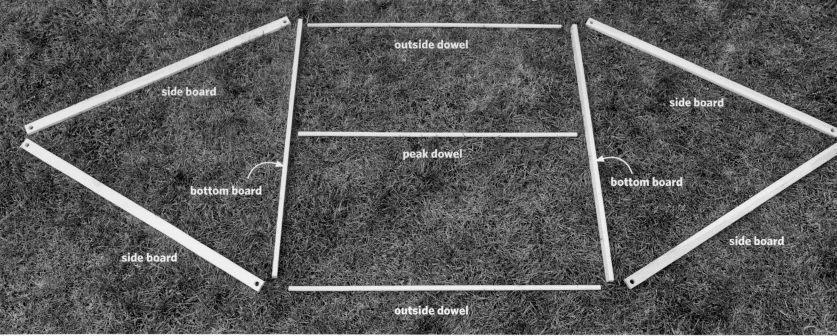

outside dowel

side board

side board

peak dowel

bottom board

bottom board

side board

side board

outside dowel

1 Clear a large space in the yard or on the floor for assembling the tent frame. Find a helper for the next steps.

2 Lay out the six boards as shown above. Each end of the tent will have one bottom board and two side boards. Lay out the three dowels as well.

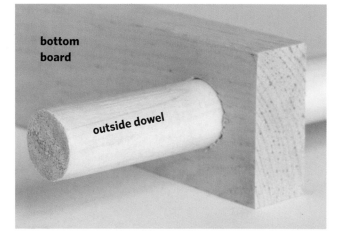

bottom board

outside dowel

3 Insert the two outside dowels through the holes in the bottom boards so that the ends of each dowel stick out a couple of inches past the bottom boards. You may have to tap the boards into place with a mallet.

4 Slide the ends of the side boards over the ends of the outside dowels, leaving about 1 inch of dowel sticking out past the side boards. Again, use a mallet if you need to.

Swing the side boards up to the peak of the tent.

5 With your helper, lift up the free ends of the side boards on either side of the assembly and swing them together so that their holes meet. The boards will now form a triangle.

peak dowel

6 Insert the ends of the third dowel through the holes in the side boards to form the peak of the tent. Make sure the dowel sticks out about 1 inch past the ends of the boards.

Idea Factory

There are tons of options for a tent cover!

Use several pieces of material to make up the sides.

Cut up old T-shirts or other pieces of fabric, knot them on a string, and drape the string over the entrance to give your tent privacy (and a colorful flair).

Make a space for a friend.

Drape a blanket, sheet, tablecloth or other large piece of fabric over the frame. This is the simplest tent of all, and the easiest to put up and take down (just in case your parents are interested in that kind of thing).

Sew a custom fabric cover

with pockets to slide the dowels through. The fabric should be 99 inches long, including 2-inch seam allowances on each side (leaving a 1-inch pocket for the dowel).

KEEP IT SIMPLE

You can also make the tent without the two bottom supports. It won't be as sturdy, but it will be easier to fold up and put away. You must add eyebolts and string to hold the sides together as shown.

Take the Tent Frame Apart

When it's time to take the tent down, just slide one side board off the peak dowel, rotate it down so that the free end lines up with the bottom board, and push it onto the outside dowel there. The tent will fold flat.

Tiny Tent

To make the tiny version, follow the same process with these supplies:

³⁄₁₆-inch brad point drill bit

6   12-inch lengths of ³⁄₈-inch square dowel

3   12-inch lengths of ³⁄₁₆-inch round dowel
    (these dowels are sometimes labeled as 0.1875 inch)

Fabric of your choice

Ribbon

You might want to buy an extra length of square dowel, as they can sometimes split when you drill them. Make sure your drill is fully up to speed before plunging it in.

Tic-Tac-Toe – To Go!

Challenge your friends in the car or at home with this nifty portable tic-tac-toe board. The dowels keep the game pieces from sliding around.

There's an unusual amount of layout work on this project, but it's a good way to practice your measuring and marking skills.

Skill Level:
Cost: $

What Do You Need?

TOOLS	MATERIALS
Safety glasses	1 piece 1×6 select pine board (at least 6 inches long)
Layout tools	1 piece ¼-inch wood dowel (at least 24 inches long)
Clamps	Sandpaper (150- and 180-grit)
Handsaw	Blue low-tack tape
Power drill	1 nail
¼-inch brad point drill bit	Paintbrush (optional)
Paintbrush (optional)	Wood glue
Mallet	9 ¼- × 1½-inch stainless steel fender washers
	Spray paint, in two colors

Mark the Board

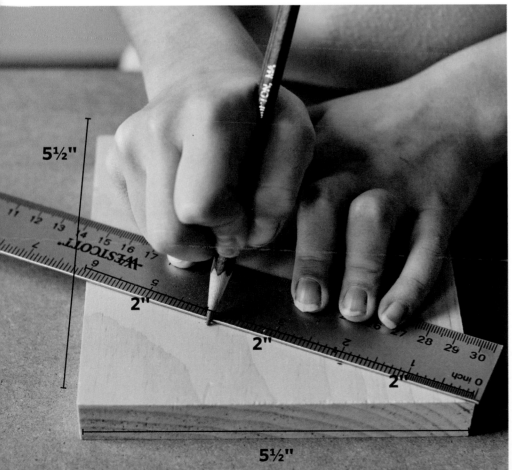

5½"

2"

2"

2"

2"

5½"

1 Measure the width of the 1×6 board. Remember the difference between nominal and actual measurements of lumber! The 1×6 board is not actually 6 inches wide. A 1×6 board is typically 5½ inches wide.

2 Tic-tac-toe boards are square, so the width and length of your game board should be equal. If your 1×6 is 5½ inches wide, measure and mark a length equal to 5½ inches, clamp the board, and cut it to that length.

3 Divide the cut board into three equal parts by using the measuring trick on page 20. Use the number 6, which can be divided by 3 into 2 inches, and mark the board every 2 inches diagonally along the length.

Mark the Board *continued*

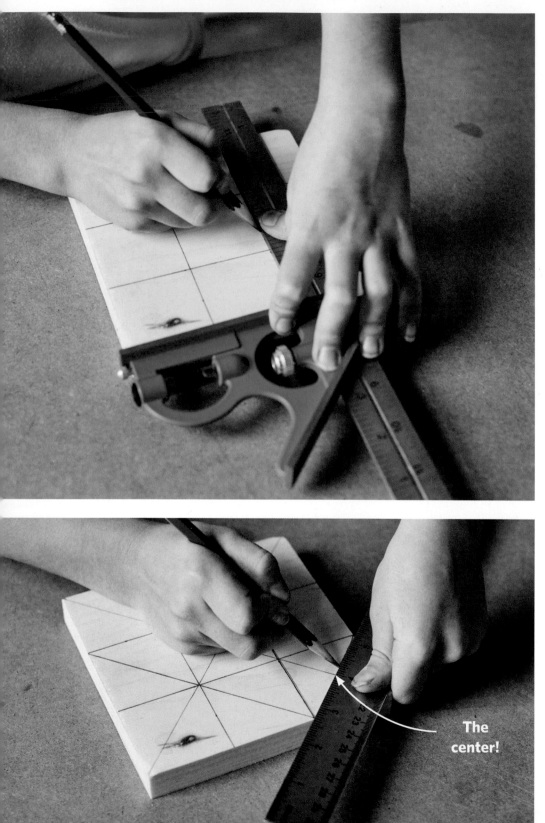

The center!

4 Square those lines across the board — that is, draw three lines down the length of the board, passing through marks you just made, using a square to make sure that the lines are straight.

5 Turn the board 90 degrees and use same method to mark lines across width. You should now have a board with nine equal squares, drawn in pencil.

6 Use the measuring trick on page 21 to mark the center of each square.

Cut the Dowel Pieces

stop line

1½"

1 Cut the dowel into nine 1½-inch lengths. You can use a narrow stock jig (page 66), if you have one. A Japanese saw is a good choice for fine cuts like these.

2 Gently sand any rough edges on the ends of the cut dowels.

Did You Know?

Tic-tac-toe is also called "Noughts and Crosses" or "X's and O's." The first three-in-a-row games were played in ancient Egypt, and an early version of tic-tac-toe was played in Rome as early as 1000 BCE.

Drill the Holes

Mark how deep the dowel will be set in the board.

1 You're going to drill a hole for a dowel piece at the center of each square. The hole should be just deep enough to hold the dowel securely. Hold a dowel against an edge of the game board with its end about halfway through the thickness of the board. Mark the spot where it crosses the edge of the board, as shown above.

2 Set the marked dowel next to the ¼-inch drill bit, with their ends aligned. Wrap a piece of blue tape around the bit at the same height as the mark on the dowel. The bottom of the blue tape will be your depth stop.

3 Clamp the game board to your workbench on top of a sacrificial board. You may have to move the clamp as you drill different parts of the board.

4 Chuck your drill with the ¼-inch drill bit. Drill each of the holes in the game board, holding the drill straight and stopping when the blue tape touches the board.

5 Sand the top and sides of the board, first with 150-grit and then with 180-grit sandpaper. (If you plan to paint the squares or lines, don't completely sand off your pencil marks.) Use a nail to loosen any sawdust in the holes, and turn the board upside down and tap it a few times with your hand to clear it out. If you want to decorate your board (see page 120), now is the time!

PRACTICE MAKES PERFECT

Before you get started drilling holes in your game board, find a scrap piece of lumber to practice drilling and stopping at the bottom of the blue tape.

Decorate the Game Board

If you want to paint or decorate your board, do it before you put in the dowels. Here's how to paint the squares in a checkerboard pattern using blue low-tack tape to mark the edges of each square. Be sure to let the paint dry before pulling off the tape for each step!

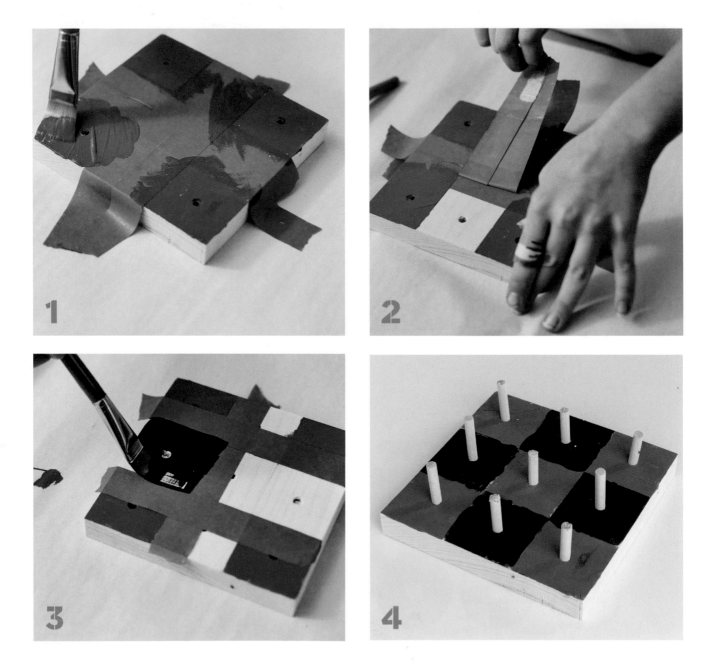

Use different types of washers or even beads for the game markers, so long as they have center holes that are a bit larger than ¼ inch so they move easily up and down the dowels.

And when you're tired of the game, turn your board into a place to hang keys or necklaces.

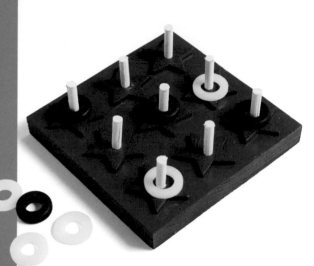

Or skip the dowels and use beads as game pieces. You could also decorate small rocks.

Idea Factory

Make these game boards with friends as a sleepover or birthday party activity!

You can precut the boards and let your friends cut the dowels and decorate the boards.

Try making a larger game board for checkers. You'll need 64 squares on the board and 24 washers.

One-Board Birdhouse

Even the birds need a comfy place to call their own. Build this one-board birdhouse in an afternoon and then stretch your creative wings by decorating it with paint, twigs, or anything else that sparks your imagination.

Exploded View

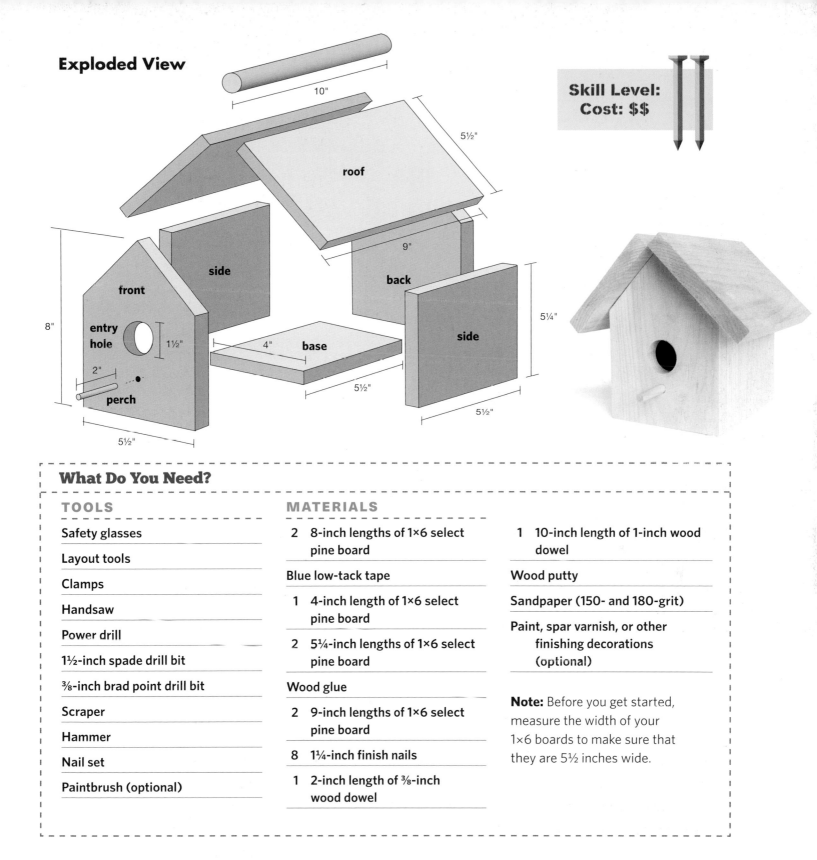

10"

5½"

roof

5½"

9"

side

back

front

8"

entry hole

1½"

2"

perch

4"

base

5½"

side

5¼"

5½"

5½"

What Do You Need?

TOOLS

Safety glasses

Layout tools

Clamps

Handsaw

Power drill

1½-inch spade drill bit

⅜-inch brad point drill bit

Scraper

Hammer

Nail set

Paintbrush (optional)

MATERIALS

2   8-inch lengths of 1×6 select pine board

Blue low-tack tape

1   4-inch length of 1×6 select pine board

2   5¼-inch lengths of 1×6 select pine board

Wood glue

2   9-inch lengths of 1×6 select pine board

8   1¼-inch finish nails

1   2-inch length of ⅜-inch wood dowel

1   10-inch length of 1-inch wood dowel

Wood putty

Sandpaper (150- and 180-grit)

Paint, spar varnish, or other finishing decorations (optional)

Note: Before you get started, measure the width of your 1×6 boards to make sure that they are 5½ inches wide.

Cut the Front and Back Pieces

Peak of the roof is at the center

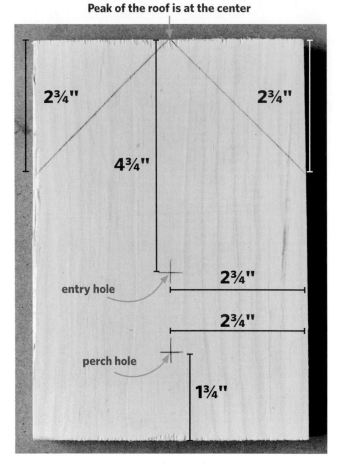

2¾"   2¾"

4¾"

entry hole   2¾"

2¾"

perch hole

1¾"

front piece

back piece

1 Find the center of the width of one of the 8-inch boards and mark the center at the top of the board. This will be the peak of the roof. On each side of the board, measure down 2¾ inches and make a mark. Use your ruler to connect each side mark with the center mark at the top. Repeat on the second 8-inch board. These are the front and back pieces of the birdhouse.

2 Mark a point on the front piece 4¾ inches down from the peak and 2¾ inches in from the side. This point is where you will drill the entry hole.

3 Mark a point on the front piece 1¾ inches up from the bottom and 2¾ inches in from the side. This point is where you will drill the hole for the perch.

front piece

saw guide

4 Set one of the marked boards on the corner of your bench, with one of the angled lines a couple of inches out from the edge of the bench. Set a scrap board along the line as a saw guide, and clamp the setup to the bench. Saw along the line.

5 Repeat the same steps to make the remaining angled cuts on the front and back pieces.

4 On the front and back pieces, mark the center of each board's thickness at the peak. (The center should be ⅜ inch in from either face of the board.) These marks are guides to help you apply glue, position the roof, and nail the roof.

5 Hammer in a 1¼-inch finish nail at the 1-inch and 3-inch marks you made on each roof piece just until the points are barely poking through. Nail directly on the lines!

6 Apply a thin line of glue to the angled edges on the birdhouse front and back pieces. Use your fingers to spread it evenly.

7 Set one of the roof pieces in place, aligning the lines on its top edge with the marks you made at the peak of the front and back pieces. Press the roof piece into place.

8 Hammer in the nails to secure the roof piece in place. Then use the nail set to tap their heads into the wood.

9 Repeat with the second roof piece.

10 Apply a small bit of glue to the end of the ⅜-inch dowel and insert it into the perch hole in the front piece.

Apply glue to the underside of the 1-inch dowel and center it in the gap between the two roof pieces. It will stick out on either side about 1 inch. Let the glue dry for about 30 minutes.

Finish Your Birdhouse

1 Fill the nail holes with a little bit of wood putty and let it dry until it feels hard to the touch. This should take about 15 minutes.

2 Sand the roof, front, back, and sides of the house, using 150-grit and then 180-grit sandpaper. Roll up the sandpaper to sand the entry hole. It's okay if it's a little rough.

3 Paint and decorate! If your birdhouse will live outdoors, finish it with either spar varnish or exterior paint.

Idea Factory

There are tons of ways to decorate your birdhouse!

Use a pencil, jacket hook, old-fashioned key, or twig instead of a dowel for the perch.

Decorate your birdhouse with found objects like bottle caps or stainless steel washers. Or add pretty beads, glass jewels, or buttons to give your birdhouse a little pizzazz.

Glue the cover of an old book onto the roof and decoupage the pages to the sides.

Attach two eyebolts to the rooftop dowel so you can hang your birdhouse.

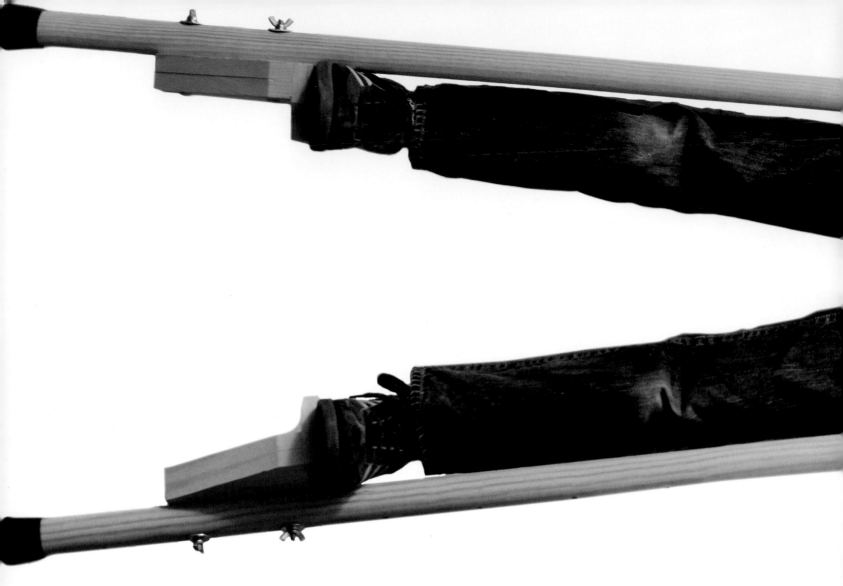

Sky-High Stilts

Wow your family and friends with these homemade stilts! They are adjustable, so you can make them higher or lower to suit your height. Heavy-duty hardware, solid footrests, and rubber feet make them sturdy and easy to use.

What Do You Need?

TOOLS

Safety glasses

Layout tools

Clamps

Handsaw

Power drill

#6 countersink bit

Phillips screwdriver

#2 Phillips screwdriver bit

¼-inch brad point drill bit

MATERIALS

4   6¼-inch lengths of 1×8 common or select pine board

2   3¼-inch lengths of 1×8 common or select pine board

Wood glue

2   72-inch (6-foot) lengths of wooden handrail

14   1¼-inch coarse-thread drywall screws

4   3½- × ¼-inch carriage bolts

Sandpaper (150-grit)

4   ¼-inch wing nuts

4   ¼-inch lock washers

4   ¼-inch fender washers

2   1¾-inch rubber feet

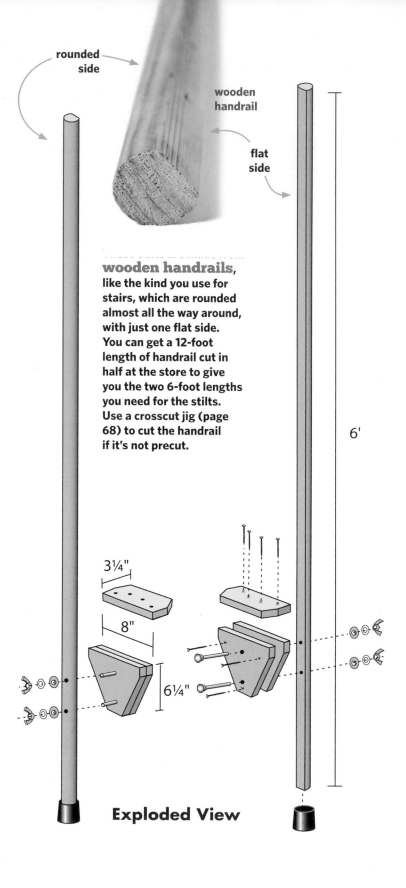

rounded side

wooden handrail

flat side

wooden handrails, like the kind you use for stairs, which are rounded almost all the way around, with just one flat side. You can get a 12-foot length of handrail cut in half at the store to give you the two 6-foot lengths you need for the stilts. Use a crosscut jig (page 68) to cut the handrail if it's not precut.

6'

3¼"

8"

6¼"

Exploded View

Mark and Cut the Base Pieces

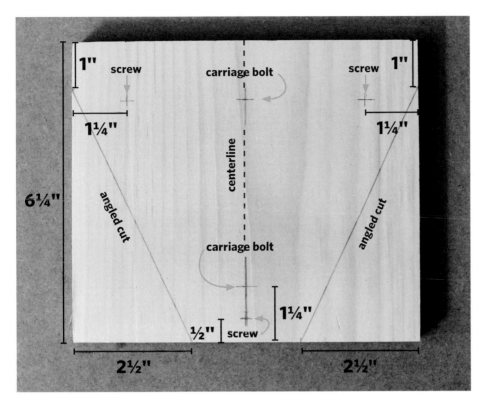

1 Measure and mark angled cutting lines on each of the 6¼-inch boards, as shown. Mark drill points for the screws and bolts on just two of the four boards, as shown.

2 Set one of the 6¼-inch boards on the corner of your bench, with one of the angled lines a couple of inches out from the edge of the bench. Set a scrap board along the line as a saw guide, and clamp the setup to the bench. Saw along the line. Then reposition the boards and make the second angled cut.

3 Make the angled cuts on the three remaining 6¼-inch boards. These four pieces are the bases for the footrests.

Mark and Cut the Footrest Pieces

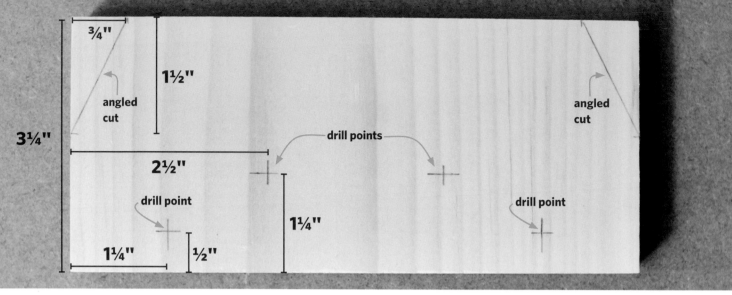

1. Measure and mark angled cutting lines on both of the 3¼-inch boards, as shown. Mark drill points for the screws on just one of the boards, as shown.

2. Set one of the 3¼-inch boards on the corner of your bench, with one of the angled lines a couple of inches out from the edge of the bench. Set a scrap board along the line as a saw guide, and clamp the setup to the bench. Saw along the line. Then reposition the boards and make the second angled cut.

3. Make the angled cuts on the second 3¼-inch board. These two pieces are your footrests.

Drill the Footrests

1 Set the unmarked footrest on your bench. Set the marked footrest on top of it, aligning all sides, and then clamp the setup to your bench.

2 Chuck your drill with the #6 countersink bit and use it to drill on the marks all the way through the top piece and into the bottom piece. Unclamp and separate the pieces.

3 Clamp the bottom footrest to your bench with the holes hanging off the edge. Use the same #6 countersink bit to finish drilling each hole, countersinking them.

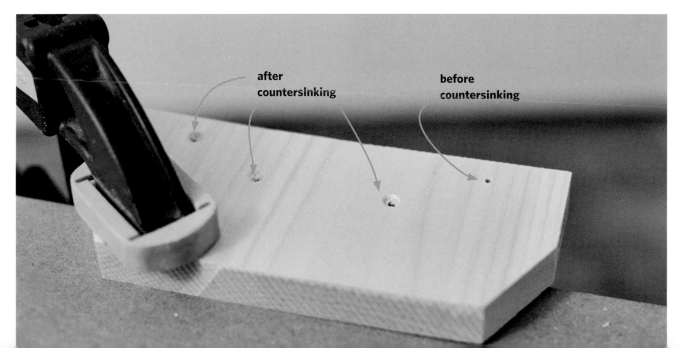

after countersinking

before countersinking

Assemble the Bases

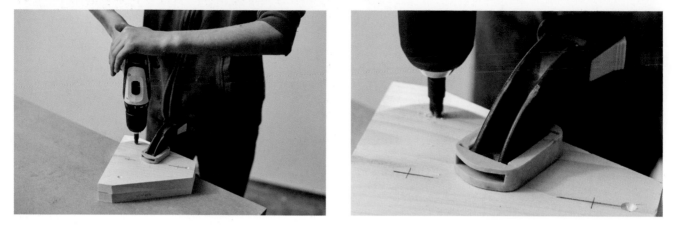

1 Of the four base pieces, two are marked with drill points and two are not marked. Clamp a marked base on top of an unmarked base, aligning all sides.

Chuck your drill with the #6 countersink bit set to 1¼ inches. Drill on the marks, through the top piece and into the bottom piece. The bit will not go all the way through the bottom piece. Then unclamp and separate the pieces.

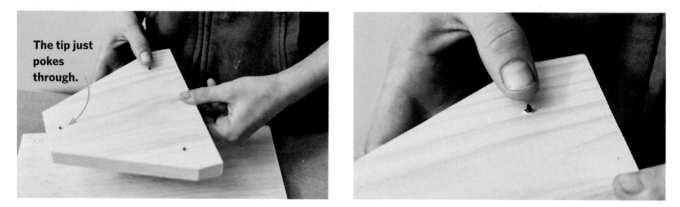

The tip just pokes through.

3 On the marked base, drive in three drywall screws with a handheld screwdriver so that their tips just poke through at the bottom.

4 Apply glue to the drilled upper face of the other base piece (not too close to the edge; try to minimize or eliminate squeeze-out).

5 Put the two pieces together and clamp them to your bench. Chuck your drill with the #2 screwdriver bit and use it to finish driving the screws into place.

6 Repeat steps 1 through 5 with the other two base pieces.

¼" holes for carriage bolts

7 Chuck your drill with the ¼-inch brad point bit. Clamp each base assembly to your bench on top of a sacrificial board and drill through it at the remaining drill points, where the carriage bolts will go.

Drill the Stilt Legs

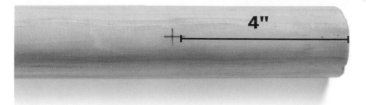

1 Mark the flat side of one handrail at 4 inches from the bottom end, centering your mark on the rail.

adult helper!

4"

support to keep the handrail level

handrail

sacrificial board

2 Clamp the handrail to your bench with a sacrificial board underneath. Set a second board of the same thickness at the other end to hold the handrail level.

3 Chuck your drill with the ¼-inch brad point bit. Drill a hole completely through the handrail at the marked point. Be sure to keep the drill perfectly vertical (perpendicular to the rail), because the bolt assembly will not work if the hole is not straight. Ask an adult for help if you need it.

4 Place one of the base pieces on the flat side of the handrail and align the bottom hole in the base with the hole you just drilled in the handrail. Insert a carriage bolt through the holes to connect the pieces. Use a marker to mark the base and the handrail with the number 1, so you know that these two parts go together.

5 Center the base on the handrail and clamp the setup in place. Use your square to make sure the top of the base is perpendicular to the rail.

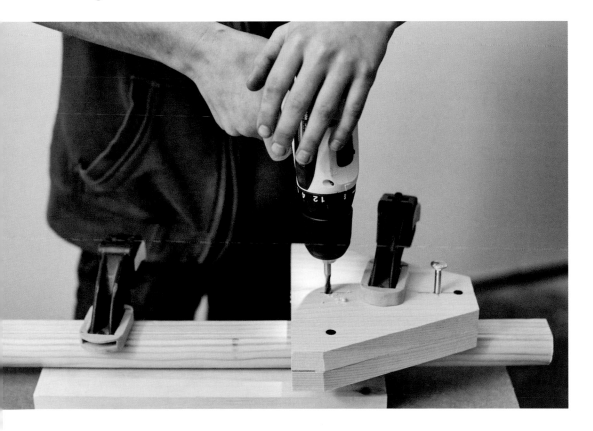

6 Still using the ¼-inch brad point bit, drill through the top hole of the base and into the handrail below. The drill bit will not be long enough to allow you to drill the hole all the way through the handrail with the base piece in the way. Just drill until you're sure you've started a hole in the handrail.

Assemble the Stilts

1 Place the #1 footrest assembly against the #1 handrail, flat sides together, so the bottom two holes are aligned.

2 Insert carriage bolts into the bottom two holes. You can use a mallet to tap the carriage bolts through the holes if they are a little tricky to push through.

3 Slide a fender washer onto the end of each bolt, followed by a lock washer and then a wing nut. Tighten the wing nuts — but not so tight that you can't loosen them when you want to raise the footrest.

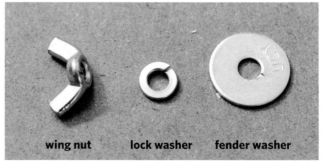

wing nut   **lock washer**   **fender washer**

4 Repeat steps 1 through 3 with the #2 footrest and handrail.

5 Fit a rubber foot onto the bottom of each stilt. If necessary, pick up the stilt and bang its foot on the ground to push the rubber foot into place.

FINISHING TOUCHES

Paint stripes around the tops of the stilts, if you'd like, or wrap them with colorful duct tape, washi tape, or glued or knotted fabric strips. This is particularly helpful if you are making more than one set, so you can tell which stilts go together.

45

Get Moving

1 Grasp the handrails on the rounded sides, with your hands pointed down.

2 Put one foot on one of the footrests and hop up onto the second footrest. Someone may have to hold the stilts for you while you steady yourself.

3 Lift up on the handrails as you move your feet. It takes lots of practice so don't get discouraged! Eventually, you'll be walking around like a pro.

Did You Know?

Stilts have been used for centuries to help people walk through marshes and swamps and to harvest fruit from trees. Shepherds have even used them to see their flocks of sheep across long distances.

My Room

Everything you need

What Do You Need?

TOOLS

Safety glasses

Layout tools

Hammer

MATERIALS

1× board, of any size or shape

Blue low-tack or masking tape

1¼-inch common nails or finish nails

String

String Thing

Skill Level:
Cost: $

Make colorful artwork as you practice using a hammer! Start with a simple design that gives you plenty of room to hammer and to fix any mistakes. As you gain confidence, try using smaller nails and tighter spacing to create your own masterpiece. You can even use cut-out photos, hand-drawn illustrations, or one of the templates at the end of this book (see pages 201–5) as a nailing guide.

Set Your Pattern

1 Set the pattern you will follow on your board. If you are planning to center your string art on the board, start by marking the center of the board, using the trick on page 21.

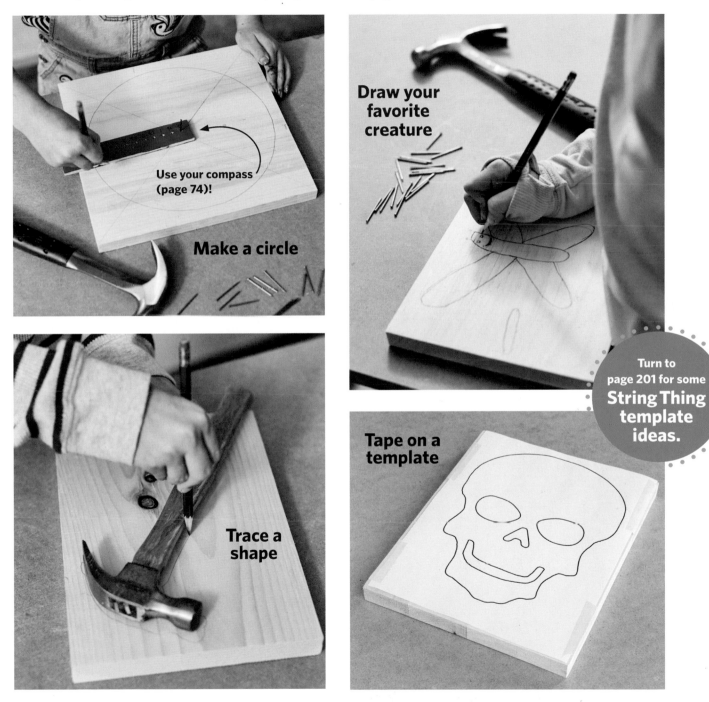

Use your compass (page 74)!

Make a circle

Draw your favorite creature

Trace a shape

Tape on a template

Turn to page 201 for some **String Thing template ideas.**

2 Mark the points on the pattern where you'll put nails. You can use a pencil to mark the points. If your pattern is an image you've taped onto your board, mark the points on the image, and then use a hammer to gently tap a nail through the paper and into the board at each point, as shown here.

Keeping at least 1½ inches between nails will make the hammering and stringing easier. Spacing them more closely together is more challenging but allows for more complex stringing patterns.

If you're working with a circle or other symmetrical shape, you may want the nails to be spaced equally along the lines you've marked. If you're working with an irregular shape, make sure you put a nail anywhere the direction changes, like corners.

Hammer the Nails

1 Hammer in a 1¼-inch nail at each of the marked points. Each nail should stand about ¾ inch to 1 inch above the board. Common nails are easier for beginners to hammer and easier to string. Finish nails work better for more complex designs with tighter spacing.

2 Look at your board from the side to check the nails. Each nail should be straight and the same height as the others. Fix any nails that are too tall or crooked.

String It!

Tie one end of the string around a nail and begin stringing. If you're using one of the templates in this book, follow the directions. Otherwise, wing it and see what you get! If you don't like it, you can always unwind and start over.

Outline images with string before
you work on the interior.

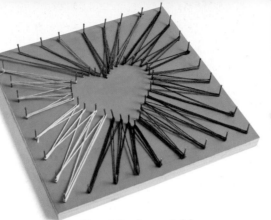

Try stringing outside
your chosen shape by hammering nails
around the edges of the board.

Idea
Factory

You can paint your board before
turning it into string art. Let it dry before you
start hammering in the nails.

Twinkle Twinkle Star

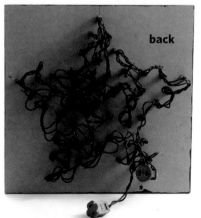

back

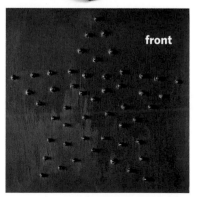

front

Light up the night with a shining star of your very own. Once you've learned the basics, you can make all kinds of twinkly shapes and words.

This simple version uses one board. The lights will stick out the back, so it's meant to lean against the wall rather than hang on it. For a hanging version, see page 160.

Mark the Board

Photocopy the star pattern. Do you notice that it's marked with dots and numbers next to them? That's so you can be sure there are exactly 50 places for you to drill, to match the 50 lights in your light string. If you accidentally make more than 50 holes, you will have to use a longer light string. Set your star pattern on the board and tape it in place.

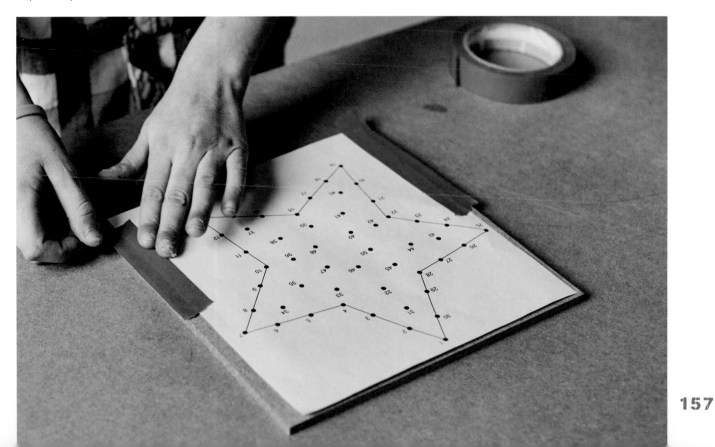

Drill the Board

test-fitting a bulb

reaming a hole

1 Find a drill bit that looks like it will match the size of the bulbs on your light string. (A $\frac{13}{64}$-inch bit seems to work for most light strings.) Chuck your drill with the bit and drill a test hole in a scrap piece of MDF.

Insert one of the bulbs from your light string in the test hole to see if it fits. The bulb should fit snugly. If it's too loose, the light will fall out. If it's just a bit too tight, try reaming the hole by inserting a screwdriver and wiggling it around to widen the hole.

Careful! To remove a light from a snug-fitting hole, push the bulb back through. Do *not* pull it by its string, or else the bulb will come apart from the string.

2 Once you have found the right size drill bit for your bulbs, you're ready to drill your star pattern. Clamp your 12-inch by 12-inch MDF board over a sacrificial board. Drill through the board at each one of the dots, drilling right through the paper pattern. This will take a while!

3 When you're done drilling, remove any paper still left on the board. Ream the holes as needed.

Finish the Board

1 Lightly sand the front and back of the board. Paint the board, if you like. Be careful not to get too much paint in the holes. (If you do, you may need to ream the holes to clear out the paint so that the bulbs will fit.)

2 Plug in the light string to make sure all of the bulbs work. Then unplug it.

3 Starting with the *female* end of the string (the end that you don't plug into the wall), insert the bulbs into the holes. Start on one side and work your way up and across the board. Finish at the bottom of the board so that the *male* end of the string (the end you plug in) can easily reach an outlet or extension cord.

4 Put your new star on your desk or a shelf and plug in the lights. Wow!

Hanging Twinkle Board

Skill Level:
Cost: $$

Once you know how to make a Twinkle Twinkle Star (page 156), you can make a twinkle board with whatever shapes and letters you want. You can also add a frame to the back so that you can hang the project. The frame sits flush against the wall and creates a space to hold the lights.

Grown-Up's Guide

The twinkle boards may require extension cords to reach from the light string to the nearest electrical outlet. Please use your judgment regarding the age of the child and the placement of the board. You might consider an extension cord with a foot pedal that powers on/off to avoid having your child repeatedly plug in and unplug the light string.

What Do You Need?

TOOLS

Safety glasses

Layout tools

Clamps

Handsaw

Power drill

Drill bit sized to the bulbs on your light strIng

Scraper

Paintbrush (optional)

MATERIALS

Blue low-tack tape

¼-inch MDF for the twinkle board

1×2 lumber for the frame

Wood glue

1½-inch finish nails

Sandpaper (150-grit)

Paint (optional)

Twinkle light strings (as many as you need)

Lay Out Your Design

1 Choose your design and get it on paper. You can handwrite it, hand-draw it, or design it digitally and print it out. Make it large enough for the lights to shine! In the example shown, the letters in the name "Kyle" are nearly 7 inches tall.

2 Cut out the shapes of your design and lay them out on your work surface. If you are spelling out a word, line up the letters along their bottom edges and space them equally. If they are too close together, they will be difficult to read when the lights are on. If they are too far apart, the lights on the light string may not reach from one letter to another. The "Kyle" letters are spaced about 1¾ inches apart.

3 When you have the shapes of your design arranged how you want them, use blue tape to secure them in place.

4 Use blue tape to mark a rectangle around your design. Leave at least 3 inches all around your design to accommodate the frame you are going to build.

Measure the inside dimensions of your rectangle.

5 The inside edges of the taped rectangle will equal the dimensions of your twinkle board. Measure the length and width of the rectangle and write down those measurements.

Set the Pattern

1 Cut a piece of ¼-inch MDF to the length and width of the rectangle you just measured. Or have the MDF cut to size at the home improvement store where you buy it.

2 Lay out your letters or shapes, centering them on your MDF. Secure the design to the board with blue tape.

3 Mark and number the drill points on your design. You should mark as many points as there are bulbs on your light string. Use a pencil to start, since it may take a few tries to get the positioning exactly right. When you're ready, go over the points with marker to make them easy to see.

NOTE: Try to put a hole anywhere the design begins or ends or wherever it changes direction. Don't worry too much about making the spacing exactly equal between the holes. When the board is lit up, no one will notice!

Drill the Board

1 Find a drill bit that will match the size of the bulbs on your light string. See page 158 for instructions.

2 Clamp your MDF board over a sacrificial board. Drill through the board at each one of the drill points that you marked, drilling right through the paper pattern.

3 When you're done drilling, remove any paper still left on the board. Ream the holes with a screwdriver as needed.

Make the Frame

1 Calculate the dimensions of your frame. The frame should be 1 inch shorter (in length and width) than the MDF board. That leaves ½ inch of space all the way around the board when it's connected to the frame.

2 Cut the frame pieces to size from the 1×2 lumber.

3 Glue, clamp, and nail the 1×2 boards together to make a rectangular frame, using 1½-inch finish nails and simple butt joints. (Follow the directions for building the frame in Storage Pegboard on page 85 if you need them.)

4 Apply glue to one side of the frame. Center it on the back of the drilled MDF board and clamp it in place. Let dry for about 30 minutes, then scrape off any excess squeeze-out.

butt joint

WOODWORKING MATH

For the "Kyle" twinkle board, the light board is 10½ inches by 18½ inches. If the frame is 1 inch smaller than the board in length and width, it will be 9½ inches by 17½ inches.

The side boards of the frame will fit in between the top and bottom boards, so you have to shorten the length of the sides to allow for the thickness of the top and bottom boards. The "Kyle" frame is made from 1×2s, which are ¾ inch thick.

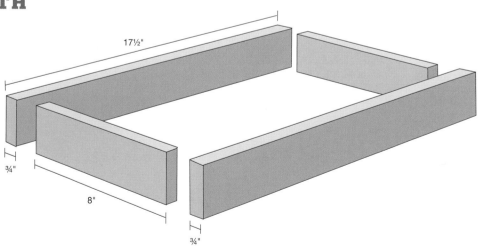

Here's the math:

¾ inch (width of top board) + ¾ inch (width of bottom board) = 1½ inches

9½ inches (height of the frame) − 1½ inches (total width of top and bottom boards) = 8 inches = length of side boards

The frame, then, is made from two 17½-inch 1×2s for the top and bottom boards and two 8-inch 1×2s for the side boards.

Finish Your Light Board

 1 Lightly sand the front and edges of the board.

 2 Paint the board and frame, if you'd like.

 3 Insert the lights, following the directions on page 159.

4 Hang your board with picture-hanging hardware or removable adhesive strips. Then light it up!

Grown-Up's Guide

It's good measuring practice for kids to start on one end of the rectangle and measure out to each point. They can check their work with this time-saving tip: set a combination square to $1/2$ inch and check their measurement on both ends. Repeat at $1^1/_2$ inches on both ends. Finally, check the middle measurement at $2^1/_2$ inches.

DIY Pencil Holder

Here's a cheerful and unique way to organize your desk or art center. Choose from two versions, depending on your skill with a saw and drill. Both the rectangle and triangle versions require the same amount of cutting and drilling, but it's more challenging to cut and drill a triangle.

What Do You Need?

TOOLS

Safety glasses

Layout tools

Clamps

Handsaw

Power drill

5⁄16-inch brad point drill bit

MATERIALS

1 5-inch length of 2×4 board
   (if you're making the rectangle version)

1 8-inch length of 2×6 board
   (if you're making the triangle version)

Blue low-tack tape

Sandpaper (150- and 180-grit)

Paint (optional)

RECTANGLE PENCIL HOLDER

Mark the Base

Stand the 2×4 board up on one edge. On the edge that's facing up, draw two parallel lines, ⅜ inch in from the sides (the faces). Starting at one end, draw lines across the board at the following points: ½ inch, 1½ inches, 2½ inches, 3½ inches, and 4½ inches. Each place where the lines cross marks a drill point.

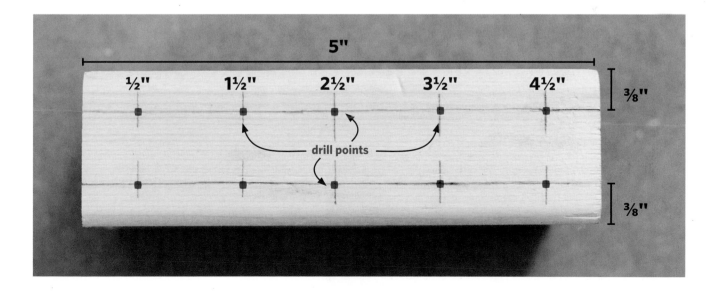

blue tape depth stop

Clamp!

Stop the drill to check your depth!

Drill the Base

1 Clamp the board securely to your bench.

2 Chuck the drill with the ⁵⁄₁₆-inch brad point bit. Set a depth stop at 1½ inches by wrapping blue tape around the bit 1½ inches from the bit's point.

3 Drill a hole in the 2×4 at one of the drill points that you marked, stopping the drill when the blue-tape depth stop touches the wood. Then test-fit a pencil. If the hole is too snug, try a larger bit.

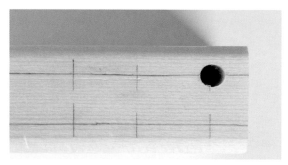

4 Drill a hole at each remaining drill point, for a total of 10 holes. Remember to let the drill get up to speed before plunging it into the wood and to keep an eye on the depth stop as you drill.

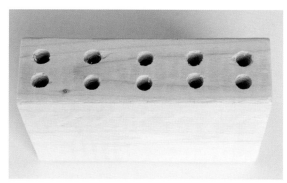

Finishing Touches

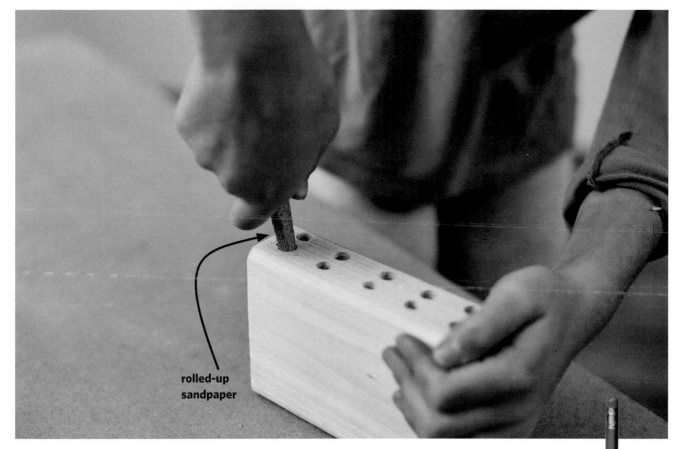

rolled-up sandpaper

1 Sand your pencil holder with 150-grit and 180-grit sandpaper. Tightly roll up a piece of sandpaper and insert it into the holes to sand off any rough edges left by the drill.

2 Finish the project with a few light coats of latex or spray paint, taking care not to let too much paint drip into the holes. If that happens, just carefully redrill the top of the hole where the paint has gone in.

TRIANGLE PENCIL HOLDER
Saw the Base

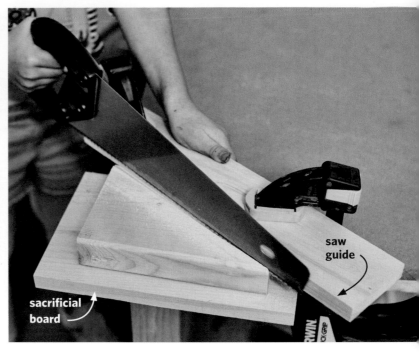

saw guide

sacrificial board

1 Draw a diagonal line from one corner of the 8-inch 2×6 to the opposing corner, using a ruler.

2 Clamp the board at the corner of your bench, on top of a sacrificial board, using two clamps. Clamp a second board on top as a saw guide. Saw through the board.

This is a big board, so sawing through it may take a while. Be patient.

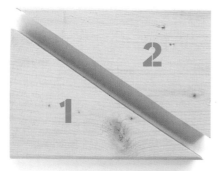

MAKE TWO!

In this project, one cut gives you two triangles. So make two pencil holders! Use one for pencils and another for pens or art brushes, or share with a friend. If you want larger holes for scissors or large brushes, use a larger drill bit and drill just a single line of holes in the center of the board.

Mark and Drill the Base

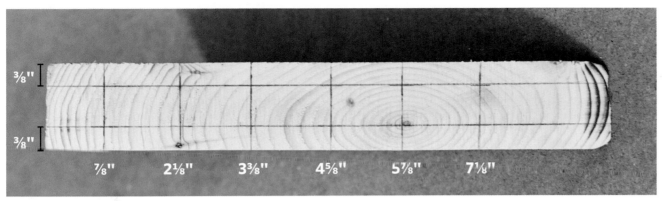

3⁄8"
3⁄8"

7⁄8" 2 1⁄8" 3 3⁄8" 4 5⁄8" 5 7⁄8" 7 1⁄8"

1 Stand the board up on its bottom edge. On the angled side that's facing up, draw two parallel lines 3⁄8 inch in from each side (face) of the board. Starting at the top, draw lines across the board at the following points: 7⁄8 inch, 2 1⁄8 inches, 3 3⁄8 inches, 4 5⁄8 inches, 5 7⁄8 inches, and 7 1⁄8 inches. Each place where the lines cross marks a drill point.

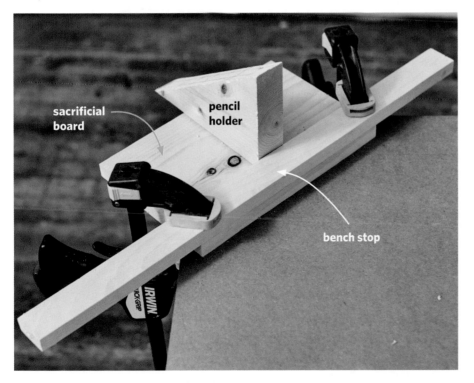

sacrificial board

pencil holder

bench stop

IRWIN

2 The base needs to be secured in place while you drill holes in it, but you can't clamp it because of its shape. Instead, clamp a narrow board on top of a sacrificial board diagonally across one corner of your bench, as shown. The narrow board will serve as a *bench stop* to hold the base in place. Set the triangle base with its back against your bench stop.

3 Chuck the drill with the 5⁄16-inch brad point bit. Set a depth stop at 1 1⁄4 inches by wrapping blue tape around the bit 1 1⁄4 inches from the bit's point.

Drill first with the bit perpendicular to the angled edge.

Then drill straight up and down.

4 Hold the drill in one hand, and hold the base securely against the bench stop with your other hand. Drill a hole in the base at one of the upper drill points that you marked. Start the hole with the drill bit perpendicular to the angled edge. Once you have a shallow hole, adjust the drill so that it's straight up and down. This takes some practice, so don't worry if your holes are a little crooked. Stop the drill when the blue-tape depth stop touches the wood.

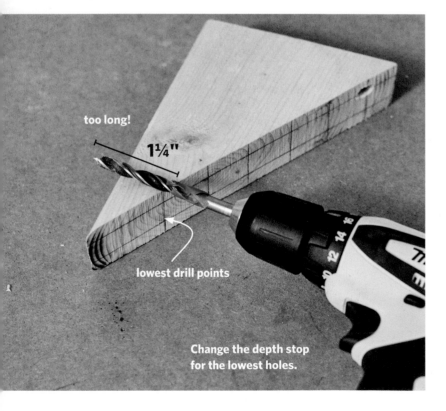

too long!

1¼"

lowest drill points

Change the depth stop for the lowest holes.

5 Test-fit a pencil in the hole you just drilled. If the hole is too snug, try a larger bit.

6 Drill a hole at all the remaining drill points except the two lowest ones, for a total of 10 holes.

7 For the lowest holes, you'll need to change the depth stop. Lay the base on its side and hold the drill bit over it, at the lowest drill points. You'll see that the current depth stop of 1¼ inches would not stop the bit before it drilled all the way through the base. When you get to these points, set a new depth stop that will stop the bit when it is halfway through the base at the lowest drill points. Then drill those last two holes.

8 Finishing touches: Sand the pencil holder, including the holes (see page 169), and decorate.

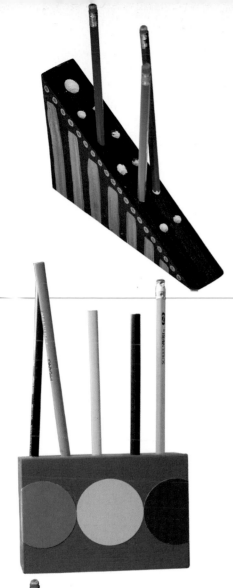

Idea Factory

Make both versions
of the pencil holder and then
invent your own ideas!

CHAPTER

6

House

Everything you need for gifts and decor

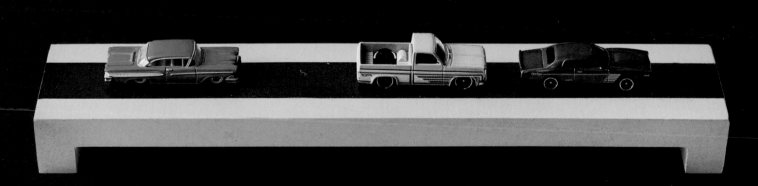

Tea Light Candleholder

The very best gifts are often those you make yourself. Imagine how proud you'll feel when you give this clever candleholder to someone special.

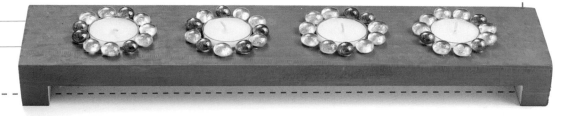
Mark the Base

1 Find the center of your 16-inch 1×4 board width, using the measuring trick on page 21. With your square, lightly draw a center line across the length of the board.

2¾"   6¼"   9¾"   13¼"

centerline

2 Measure and mark the following points on the center line you just drew, starting from the left end of your board and making small crosses at each point: 2¾ inches, 6¼ inches, 9¾ inches, and 13¼ inches.

3 Clamp the board on both ends, on top of a sacrificial board. Make sure none of your cross marks are covered.

Drill the Base

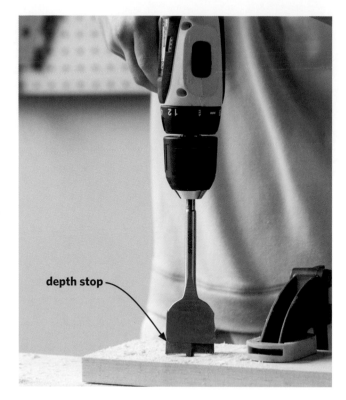

depth stop

2 Chuck your drill with the 1½-inch spade bit. Your holes should only be about ½ inch deep, so you need a depth stop. You can use blue tape to mark a depth stop on the bit (see page 34), but the spade bit will spin so fast that it will be hard to see the tape; stop the drill frequently to make sure you're not going too deep. It's okay if the tip of the bit goes all the way through the wood — no one will see it!.

It spins fast!

1 Chuck your drill with the ⅛-inch drill bit. Drill shallow pilot holes in the center of each cross mark. The drill bit should enter the wood just enough to create a starting point for the spade bit.

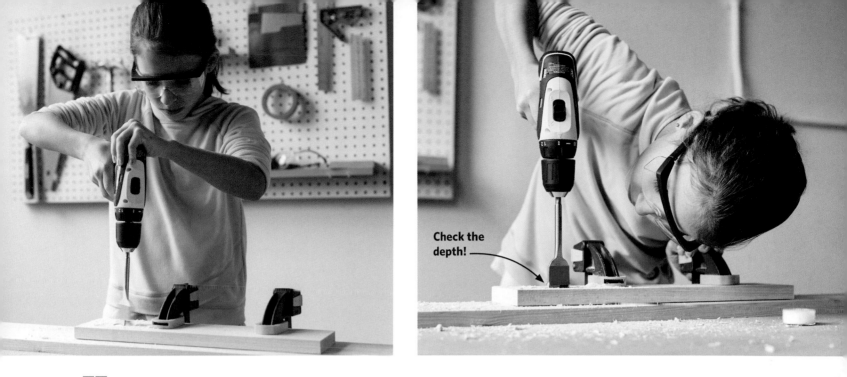

Check the depth!

3 Drill one of the 1½-inch holes, being sure to let the drill come up to full speed before plunging the bit in. As you drill, move the bit in and out of the hole to clear out the sawdust. Stop often to check the depth of the hole.

4 Test-fit the hole by putting in one of the tea light candles to see if you like the depth. You can always drill more deeply, but you can't make the hole more shallow, so it's a good idea to test it as you go.

5 Ream (widen) the hole, if necessary. Most tea lights are about 1½ inches in diameter, but that may be such a tight fit in a 1½-inch hole that it's hard to insert and remove them. To ream a hole, put the spade bit back in the hole. Turn on the drill and — *without applying downward pressure* — gently rock the bit back and forth. The bit will nibble away at the edges but won't make the hole any deeper.

6 Drill the remaining three holes, and ream them if necessary.

Test the fit.

TEST TIME

Good woodworkers take the time to "test" new tools and techniques. On this project, you're using a large bit and trying not to drill too deeply with it. Test it a few times on a clamped piece of scrap wood until you feel comfortable with the process.

Attach the Feet

1 Set the base on your bench, with the holes facing down. Set the 1-inch 1×4 pieces next to it, with their wide faces facing up. These small blocks are the feet.

2 Apply a thin line of glue to one of the wide faces of each foot block. Put the glue line a little bit closer to one edge than the other; this will be the inside edge, and if you have any squeeze-out, the glue will be on the underside of the candleholder.

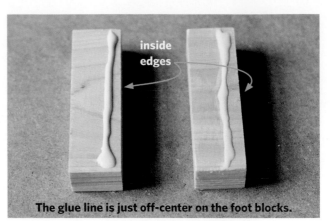

The glue line is just off-center on the foot blocks.

3 Place one foot block on one end of the base, glue side down, with the inside edge facing inward. Align the end and edges. Clamp the joint, realigning as needed. Do the same to attach the other foot block to the opposite end of the base.

4 Wipe off any glue on the inside of the base. If some glue squeezes out on the outside, leave it and scrape it off after 30 minutes. Leave the clamps on for 30 minutes.

Sand Your Work

1 Sand the candleholder first with 150-grit and then 180-grit sandpaper. If you plan to stain it, also sand with 220-grit to make the surface really smooth.

2 Roll or fold up a piece of sandpaper and rub it against the insides and bottoms of the holes. These will be covered by the candles, so it's okay if they are a little rough.

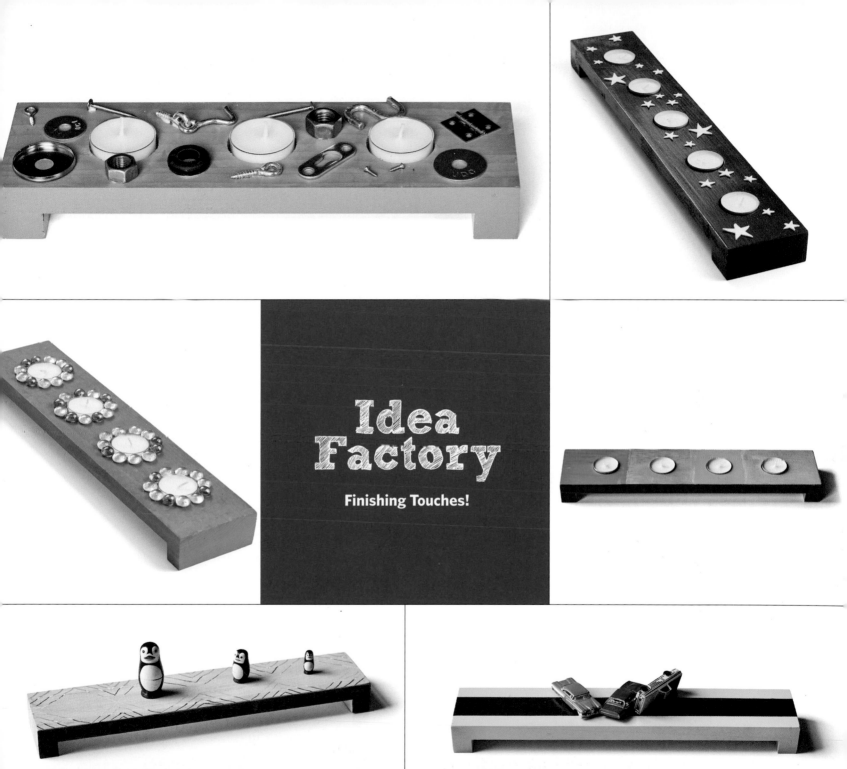

Idea Factory

Finishing Touches!

Keep It Simple

The trickiest part of this project is drilling the large holes. You can skip that step for now and instead make a pretty stand for votive candles, small flower vases, or knicknacks. As your confidence grows, come back and give the holes a try.

Clock Time

Measure, cut, and drill a simple hexagon or square clock face and then decorate it as you please. The square version requires less measuring and fewer cuts, so it's a good place to start. But read through the instructions for both before choosing one.

Grown-Up's Guide

Young woodworkers can start with a 9-inch-square piece, but it's good layout and sawing practice to start with a larger board and cut it down. This project can be customized to any size of clock.

HEXAGON CLOCK
Lay Out the Hexagon

1 Mark the center of the MDF board, using the diagonal-line trick on page 21.

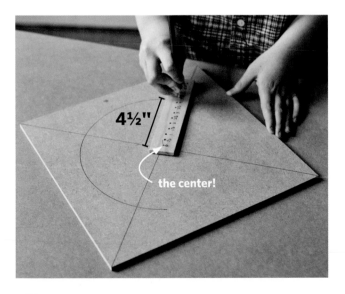

4½"

the center!

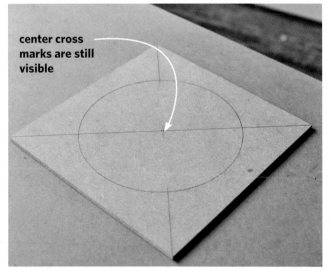

center cross marks are still visible

 2 Use a compass to draw a circle with a 4½-inch radius, centered on the MDF board. The diameter of the circle is 9 inches.

3 Erase just *one* of the diagonal lines, as shown, leaving the center cross mark.

Lay Out the Hexagon *continued*

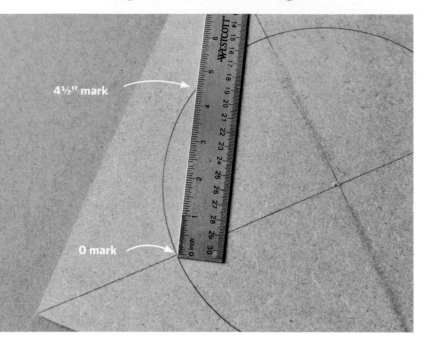

4 Set your ruler so that the 0 is on the point where the diagonal line crosses the circle. Adjust the ruler until the 4½-inch mark is also on the circle. Draw a line.

5 Move your ruler so that the 0 is on the point where the line you just drew crosses the circle. Adjust the ruler until the 4½-inch mark is also on the circle. Draw a second line.

6 Repeat four more times, for a total of six lines that mark out a hexagon inside the circle. Measure carefully! If you get to the last line and it doesn't match up with the beginning of the first line, you may have to redo one or more lines.

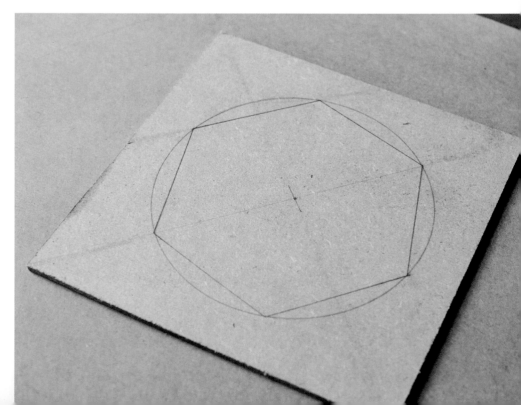

Saw the Clock Face

The cut line is extended across the board.

1 Clamp the board to your bench so that one of the 4½-inch lines is about 2 inches past the side of the bench. Set a ruler on that line and use a pencil to extend the line over the face of the board, as a sawing guide. If you like, you can also clamp a board along the line as a saw guide.

2 Saw the board along the extended line.

3 Adjust, reclamp, and saw the board to cut along the remaining five lines. In each case, extend the cut line across the face of the board to serve as a sawing guide.

Drill a Hole for the Clock Movement

1 Clamp your clock face to a sacrificial board. Chuck the drill with the ⁵⁄₁₆-inch brad point bit. Drill through the center of the face.

2 Test-fit your clock movement by inserting it into the hole. If the hole is too small, you may have to ream it with a screwdriver (see page 158) or try a larger drill bit. It's okay if the hole is a little too big because the clock movement will be tightened down onto the face.

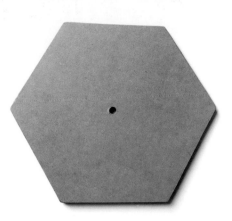

Finishing Touches

1 Sand your clock face smooth with 150-grit and 180-grit sandpaper.

2 Paint, decorate, and number the face. This is the creative part! Hand-write numbers with permanent marker or paint pens, or buy premade numbers and glue them in place. Start with the numbers on the top, bottom, and middle (that's the 3, 6, 9, and 12), and then space the rest of the numbers evenly between them. The more precise you are, the more accurate the clock will be.

3 Follow the directions that come with the clock movement to attach it and insert batteries. Then hang your new clock, using the hole provided on the clock movement.

SQUARE CLOCK

1 Mark the center of the MDF board, using the diagonal-line trick on page 21.

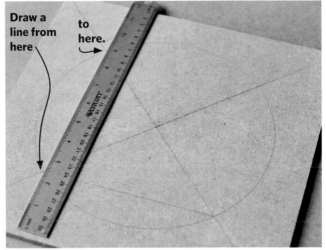

Draw a line from here ➜ to here.

2 Use a compass to draw a circle with a 4½-inch radius, centered on the MDF board. The diameter of the circle is 9 inches.

3 Place your ruler on a point where one of the diagonal lines crosses the circle. Adjust the ruler so that it lines up with the next point where a line crosses the circle. Draw a line to connect the points.

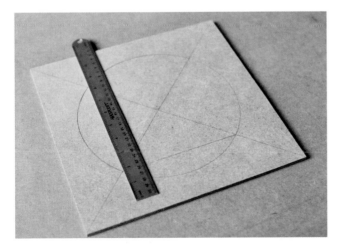

4 Repeat three more times to complete the square.

5 Follow the directions on pages 185 and 186 to cut, drill, and finish your square clock. Position the numbers every 2½ inches along each edge of the square face.

Mighty Message Board

Help keep your family organized and on time! Use the skills and design you learn here to build other clever organizers for your room or other places in your home.

What Do You Need?

TOOLS

Safety glasses

Paintbrush

Layout tools

Clamps

Miter box and saw

Power drill

#2 Phillips screwdriver bit

Hot glue gun

Rag

MATERIALS

1   17½- × 23½-inch piece of ¼-inch MDF

Chalkboard paint

2   25-inch pieces of 1¼-inch-wide wall trim
     of your choice

2   19-inch pieces of the same 1¼-inch-wide wall trim

1   scrap board, sized for miter box
     (if needed to clamp the miter box to your bench)

2   1¼-inch coarse-thread drywall screws
     (if needed to clamp the miter box to your bench)

Blue low-tack or packing tape

Wood filler

Sandpaper (150- and 180-grit)

Paint or stain (optional)

Hot glue

BUILDING THE FRAME WITH BUTT JOINTS

This message board features a frame with mitered corners. If you don't have a miter box, or if you want an
easier method, you can make the frame from 1×2 lumber and use butt joints at the corners.

Cut the lumber into four pieces:

- Two 24-inch lengths

- Two 15-inch lengths

Assemble the frame as shown
below, gluing the joints and clamping
them until they're dry. If your clamps
aren't long enough, secure the joints
with packing tape instead.

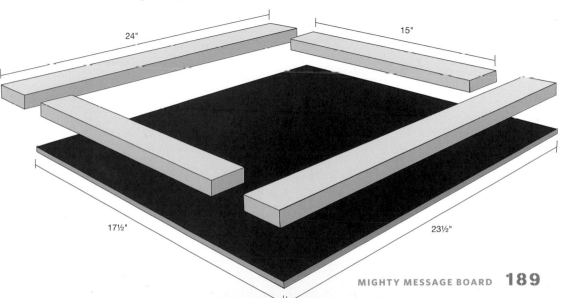

Paint the Board

Paint the MDF with at least two coats of chalkboard paint. Craft stores carry this kind of paint in black and other colors.

Set Up Your Miter Box

Screw the miter box to a long board so you can clamp it.

Clamp your miter box to your bench, if you can. Most miter boxes don't have enough space to let you clamp them. If you can't clamp yours, chuck your drill with a #2 Phillips screwdriver bit and use it to drive drywall screws through the miter box and into a board that's approximately the same width as the miter box and at least 1 foot longer on each end. Then clamp that board to your bench on either end.

THE MITER CUTS

You build your message board frame from four lengths of 1¼-inch-wide wall trim. Two pieces are 19 inches long, and the other two are 25 inches long. The steps on the following pages will show you how.

First Cuts

With your first round of miter cuts, you'll trim one end of each board at a 45-degree angle.

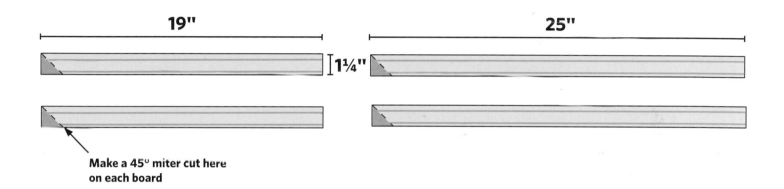

Make a 45° miter cut here
on each board

Second Cuts

With your second round of cuts, you'll trim the opposite ends at a 45-degree angle so that two
19-inch boards are now 18 inches on their longest side, and the 25-inch boards are now 24 inches.

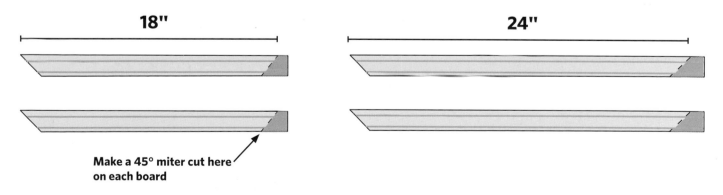

Make a 45° miter cut here
on each board

Make the First Miter Cuts

1 Set a 25-inch piece of trim in the miter box so that the flat face of the trim is on the bottom of the box and the flat edge of the trim is up against the *near fence* (the vertical side of the box that is nearest to you). Position the piece so that its corner just meets the 45-degree kerf slot in the miter box. (You want to cut off as little of the trim as possible in this cut.)

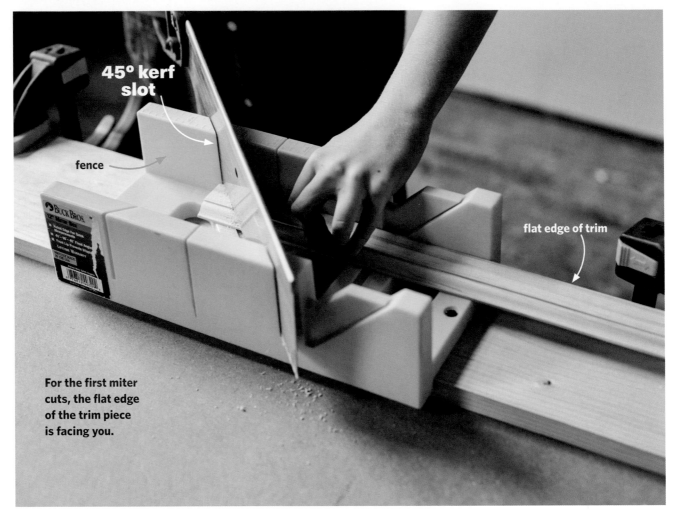

45° kerf slot

fence

flat edge of trim

For the first miter cuts, the flat edge of the trim piece is facing you.

2 Hold the trim firmly against the near fence and the bottom of the miter box with your free hand, and cut through the trim piece at a 45-degree angle. Use the saw that comes with the miter box; the stiff spine helps keep the saw blade straight.

3 Repeat with the second 25-inch length and both 19-inch lengths of trim.

Make the Second Miter Cuts

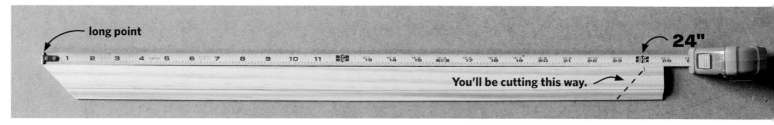

long point

24"

You'll be cutting this way.

1 Measure and mark one of the longer trim pieces to 24 inches. Measure from the long point of the angled end.

2 Place the marked piece back in the miter box, again with the flat face on the bottom. Set your saw blade in the 45-degree kerf slot so that it is angled in the **opposite direction** from the miter cut you already made. Position the trim piece so that the saw falls right on the mark you made at 24 inches.

3 Once the trim piece is in position, hold it there while a helper clamps a stop block in place to secure the trim piece. Then make the cut.

4 Repeat with the second long trim piece.

5 Repeat with the shorter pieces, cutting them to 18 inches as measured from long point to long point.

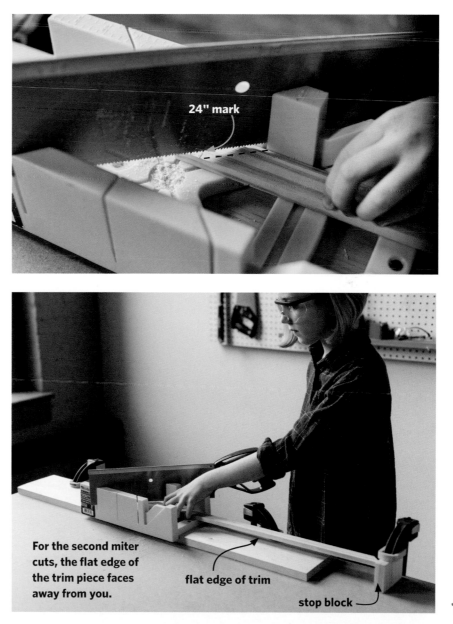

24" mark

For the second miter cuts, the flat edge of the trim piece faces away from you.

flat edge of trim

stop block

193

Assemble the Frame

1 Set up the boards to form a rectangle on the floor, with the decorative side facing up. See how the angle is opposite on either end of each board? That's so the ends will fit together to make a corner. It's okay if the corners aren't perfect! Miters are tough to do, and you can fill in any gaps with wood filler.

tape

tape

2 "Unfold" the frame so that the pieces are aligned in straight line. At the three places where the four pieces of wood touch, put a piece of blue tape or packing tape on the flat edge of the trim, as shown, and press the wood into the tape.

3 Working with your helper, roll the pieces as a group onto their back sides, so that the taped edge is now on the floor.

4 Apply glue to each raw miter-cut edge with your finger. Let the glue sink in a bit, then apply a little more.

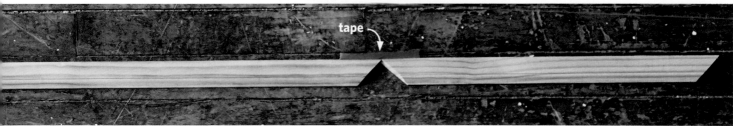

tape

Assemble the Frame *continued*

5 Starting at one end, close each joint, pulling the tape tightly around the pieces to secure the joint.

6 When you get to the last joint, hold the pieces together and have a helper put tape on it.

7 If you're planning to paint the frame, wipe away (gently) any glue squeeze-out. Otherwise, let it dry for 30 minutes, then scrape off the glue. Let the glue dry overnight before moving to the next step.

NOTE: These edge-to-edge joints with a small surface area are not very strong. Be very gentle with your frame until it's attached to the board. If a joint breaks apart, sand off any glue in the joint and glue it back together.

8 The next day, fill any gaps in the mitered joints with wood filler and let it dry.

Wood filler fills the gaps!

9 Sand the frame with 150-grit and 180-grit sandpaper. Stain the frame, or paint it with latex or spray paint, if you want. Let the finish dry.

Attach the Chalkboard

1 Lay the frame facedown on your bench on top of a piece of newspaper or cloth. Use 150-grit sandpaper to rough up the back of the frame. Wipe off all of the dust with a clean rag.

2 Center the chalkboard on top of the frame.

3 Load the hot glue gun with glue and plug it in near your work table. If you need help using it, ask a grown-up!

4 Lift up one side of the chalkboard and apply a line of hot glue along the middle of the trim pieces beneath it. Quickly set the board back in place, lining up all of the corners of the frame with your marks. Press firmly on the board until the glue cools.

5 Gently lift up the other end of the board and apply glue along all edges. If any of the first glued edge lifts up a bit, just reglue it! Press firmly on the board until the glue cools.

6 Hang your new board with picture-hanging hardware or removable hanging strips. Write a big "thank you" to your helper!

NAILING THE FRAME

If you have a thick frame, you may be able to clamp the pieces to your bench and use tiny brad nails to fasten the chalkboard to the frame, instead of hot gluing. Nail through the chalkboard and into the thickest parts of the frame.

Paint a piece of metal to make a magnetic board.

Make a board with precut radiator cover — a finished sheet-metal panel with decorative holes — and hang items with small hooks.

Idea Factory

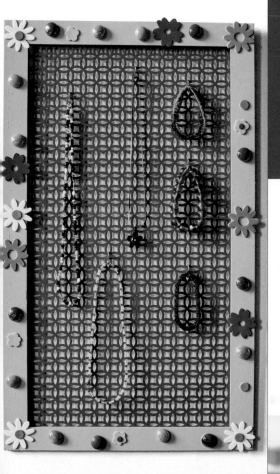

Apply whiteboard paint instead of chalkboard paint to create a dry-erase board.

Swap out the MDF for corkboard and use thumbtacks to hang jewelry, notes, or medals.

Makers' Market

Use your new skills to make money for yourself or for your favorite charity.

Where Do I Start?

Choose one or two projects from the book; these will be your products to sell. Start with projects that don't cost much — or take too long — to make. The less money you have to spend to build your products, the more profit you make!

Sales price – the cost of materials = your profit

Where Do I Sell?

School craft fairs, a craft stand in front of your house, holiday events — wherever you can get permission to sell your product. Arrange your products nicely on a table with a small sign that explains why you're raising money. Your customers will like knowing more about you.

How Much Do I Charge?

Try to keep the price under $10. You'll sell more items if the price is low, and after your first market, you'll know which of your products are most popular. People love getting a deal, so consider giving a discount if they buy more than one.

String Thing Templates

Use these templates for the project on page 150. Use Twinkle Twinkle Star for the project on page 156.

Twinkle Twinkle Star

Balloons

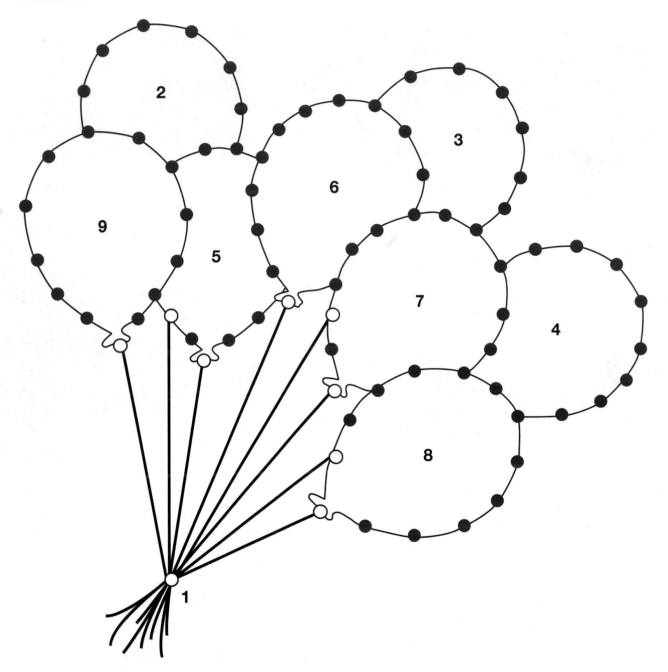

1 String the balloon strings in white, leaving a tail for each string as you wrap it around point #1.

2 Using different colors, string the balloons in numerical order as shown. The more you string, the more colorful the finished project will be!

Baseball

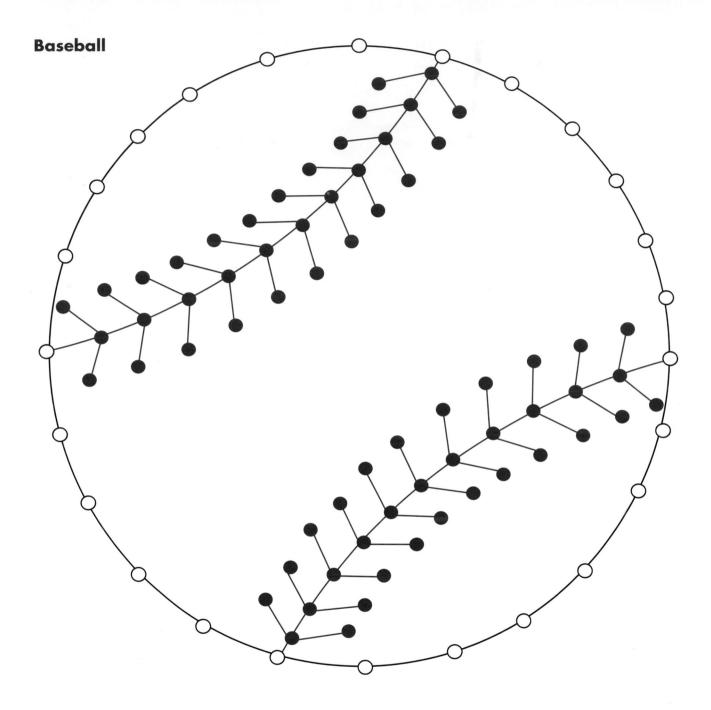

 1 Outline the outer circle of the baseball in white.

2 Fill in the entire circle in white, criss-crossing back and forth between all the nails. This provides a nice white background for the red seams.

3 On the seam marks, push the white string down to the bottom of the nails to make room for the red string.

4 String the seams in red along the lines, as shown. The more string you use, the thicker the seams will be.

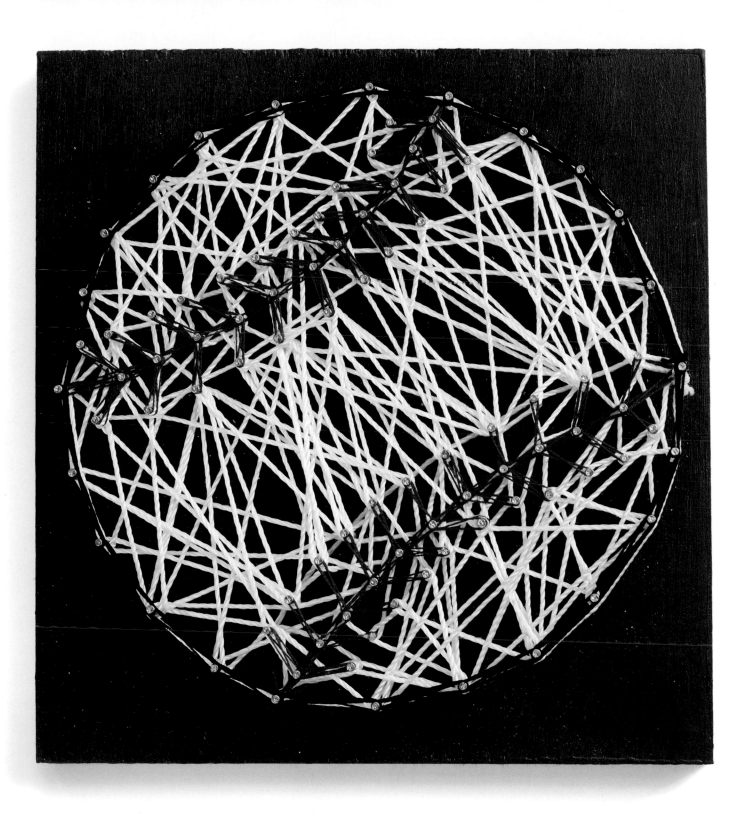

Index

METRIC CONVERSION CHART
LENGTH

TO CONVERT	TO	MULTIPLY
inches	millimeters	inches by 25.4
inches	centimeters	inches by 2.54
inches	meters	inches by 0.0254
feet	meters	feet by 0.3048

Become a Well-Rounded Maker
with More Books from Storey

by Deanna F. Cook

Bakers-in-training will learn how to knead dough, make biscuits, decorate cookies, and produce the perfect piecrust. These 50 easy-to-follow recipes include popular picks like blueberry muffins, brownies, birthday cake, bread sticks, and crispy cheese crackers.

by Deanna F. Cook

This fresh, fun cookbook teaches basic cooking techniques in kid-friendly language, with dozens of recipes (and stickers!) for favorite foods like French toast, homemade granola, Buffalo chicken fingers, tortilla chips, and much more.

by Amie Petronis Plumley & Andria Lisle

Kids can complete these 21 inspired hand-sewing projects with minimal supervision. Step-by-step photographed instructions teach basic sewing skills and how to put them to use making pillows, dolls, blankets, totes, and more.

by Nicole Blum & Catherine Newman

Create, hack, or customize! Step-by-step directions show kids the basics of how to sew, embroider, knit, crochet, weave, and felt. They can then use their new skills to hand-make cool bracelets, backpacks, merit badges, keychains, and more.
